PEACOCKS AND COMMAS

PEACOCKS AND COMMAS

The Best of the *Spectator* Competitions

chosen and presented by
Joanna Lumley

illustrated by Michael Heath

THE BODLEY HEAD
LONDON   SYDNEY
TORONTO

983045

British Library Cataloguing
in Publication Data
Lumley, Joanna
Peacocks and commas:
the best of the Spectator competitions.
1. English wit and humour
I. Title   II. Heath, Michael
828'.91407'08   PN6175
ISBN 0 370 30976 6

This selection and illustrations
© The Bodley Head 1983
Foreword © Joanna Lumley 1983
Printed in Great Britain for
The Bodley Head Ltd
9 Bow Street, London WC2E 7AL
by Redwood Burn Ltd, Trowbridge
Set in Linotron 202 Sabon
by Wyvern Typesetting Ltd, Bristol.
First published 1983

CONTENTS

For
Kitty Thomson

FOREWORD

The only competition in which I ever won a prize invited us to write an essay describing an imaginary place. Not reading the instructions properly, I set off with a feverish ten-year-old's enthusiasm and submitted a whole book entitled *Triple Peak Island*. It had eleven chapters, a very strong story-line, I thought, and it came with full-colour illustrations throughout. I drew tame zebras, pirates, forest fires, giant shells and, of course, the Triple Peaks themselves: strangely symmetrical mountains with pink snow clinging grimly to their summits. Aghast at my zeal, the judges gave me a glass swan. Mercifully, the entrants in the *Spectator* competitions are of a very different calibre; no drawings at all, and each composition responding with thrilling accuracy to the problem posed by Jaspistos or Charles Seaton and, very occasionally, A. N. Other. I was given the task of making a selection from the winning entries; about three thousand gems of invention at the back of each issue. Photocopies were made: I did some, and when my arms became as brawny as Arnold Schwarzenegger's, I feebly handed over to one Sam McAllister. He pumped iron for another seven and a half years (of competitions, that is) and I arrived home with several hundred slices of inky reproductions. I started to read. I read for hours, which turned to days and weeks; I scuttled some and shuffled through others, riffling through these and giggling through those. Not having much of a mind for filing, I started to stack them about in rough piles—God, love, travel, food—and I spread the piles in easy-to-get-at heaps, which went all over the drawing-room and through the hall into my writing room. I tiptoed daintily through them for days, mauve in the face from bending down to determine whether Shakespeare and aphorisms had become commingled. Great Powers! What a task! Who are the people who compete in these competitions? I am now aware that there are souls in these comfortable islands whose boffin-domed heads are surely taken about on plates like the Mekon, whose literary knowledge is so encyclopaedic that their fingers are probably paper-thin from turning pages. Many names appear again and again, and some only once. This book is theirs, and my grateful thanks go to them all for the hours of fun and silliness they have afforded me. I can modestly claim to have bettered myself in the process: I have been introduced to the paracrostic and the pantoum, and wish to point out that the whole of this foreword has been written in lipogrammatic form—the missing letter is *q*.

JOANNA LUMLEY

Confessions of a Competition Addict:

I got hooked when a friend, his eyes unnaturally bright, stood me a double Scotch. 'You're flush,' I said enviously. 'I've just won a literary competition,' he told me. After that it was a deep slide into hell.

I started with the *New Statesman*, then moped on to the hard stuff in the *Spectator*. I suffered withdrawal symptoms when *Punch* stopped the Toby competitions. Nothing else mattered but that weekly fix. I even started 'fagging' (using several pseudonyms).

I sold everything and filled the house with reference books. I lost my job. My wife left me. Then a fellow-addict introduced me to Competitors Anonymous. Now whenever I feel the urge a member of CA comes and sits with me until the deadline is past.

But I know I shall never be wholly cured. All I can ever say is, 'I haven't entered for a competition *this* week.'

(Roger Woddis)

The
Happiest Days
of Your Life

*Competitors were asked to complete a poem beginning 'It looks like a
season of Peacocks and Commas':*

It looks like a season of Peacocks and commas,
It looks like a winter of colons and *Lear*;
That Abbey's a Nightmare; they never love Thomas,
Nor old *Jude the Obscure* by Hardy the drear.

It looks like a season of essays and *Emma*;
And creative writing, which means they can't spell;
There's *The Lord of the Flies, The Doctor's Dilemma*,
And then *Paradise Lost*, which they find sheer hell.

It looks like a season of précis and *Dombey*,
And dull comprehension they don't understand;
I dictate all the notes, each writes like a zombie,
The Sixth's got its Melville, which ought to be grand.

Now yet one more season of grim punctuation,
Of poems they scoff at, of novels they hate,
Of screaming and chalk-dust and mental frustration;
I'm retiring next summer, and hardly can wait.
                              (E. O. Parrott)

'Ride a Cock-Horse'

A slow coming we had of it,
Just at the worst time of the year:
In spring is the wintriest weather.
With the cock-horses fretful and wanting their sugar,
There were times when we began to wonder
If there was such a place as Banbury.
We would have abandoned the search
But for the promise of the Cross; so we continued
And arrived at evening, not a moment too soon,
Finding the lady; it was (you may say) satisfactory.
Certainly there were bells on her feet, and such bells
Tinkling and partly tinkling,
And her fingers were heavy with many rings.
Had we been drawn here by memory before birth or curiosity?
In our ignorance is our understanding.
                                    (E. O. Parrott)

There was an old sailor who went out to sea
In a lovely big boat, and had honey for tea.
The crew were all dressed up in satin and silk,
And they carried a cargo of cornflakes and milk.
One day, when he'd got nothing better to do,
He shot a big birdie, and that killed the crew.
The ship wouldn't move, he was stuck on the deck
With a 'normous great albatross tied round his neck.
The water ran out, and so did the gin;
Can you imagine the state he was in?
There was an old sailor who went out to sea—
I'm ever so glad it was him and not me.
                                    (I. C. Snell)

Competitors were invited to describe a bizarre incident at a fictional school involving, amongst other things, botulism:

At st custards the skolars unpack wot there fond maters have speshully sent. As Peason eat roten chese, Fotherington-Tomas open tin of samon, he is uterly wet. He says 'oh goody' and then he suddenly stifen.

I note rust-spek on his tin. Lukily, we hav done wizard biol lesson on FATUL DISEESES and i xpertly kno this is the dreded BOTTULISM. Siezing samon, i zoom to headmaster with practiced smirk on my inocent hem-hem lips.

'Sirsir have some samon' I say swetely (the words doth trip of my lip ect) which he do v. gredily.

WHOOSH I run at spede of lite (e = mcc² eh wot?) to announce DOOM of Grimes to fellow skolars.

Chiz.

Fotherington-Tomas still look blank, but suddenly say 'i was entranced by yonder clouds beauty. Were is my samon molesworth?'

Another briliant MASTER-PLAN foiled!
                (Ellen Brigwell)

A schoolchildren's battle song:

The children's flag is black and blue,
To show what we're subjected to,
We'll give attention to the old
But not the right to knock us cold.
Then raise the pupils' standard high,
We'll learn from Marx and Chou En-lai,
Though Fascists flinch and Tories jeer,
We'll keep the kids' flag flying here!

With knees uncovered swear we all
To write our slogans on the wall,
Come lousy grub and grotty gym,
This song shall be our battle-hymn.
Then raise the pupils' standard high,
We'll never wear the old school tie,
Though grown-ups wince and papers smear,
We'll keep the kids' flag flying here!

We'll educate the powers-that-be
In friendship and fraternity,
And teach our comrades not to grass
On fellow-workers in the class.
Then raise the pupils' standard high,
And down with every Captain Bligh!
Though parents groan and teachers fear,
We'll keep the kids' flag flying here!
(Roger Woddis)

Creatures Great and Small

A bird unenthusiastically addresses Man:

O Poet Gray, your Elegy won't do.
'The moping owl'—Hoots, mon, that wasn't true.
I was a hoping owl. I had in view
A more romantic aim—to wit, to woo.

'Complain', did I? I'm not a grouse. And who
Would wish for solitary reigns, when two
Are much more fun than one? I thought men knew
How best to spend the night—to wit, to woo.

Far ruder than your rude forefathers, you
Delayed my mate. She was then overdue.
She knew a poet 'neath our rendezvous
Would spoil our little game—to wit, to woo.

And there you sat, scribbling and crossing through.
Had you no other better things to do?
Darkness was left to us as well as you.
The ploughman went. Why didn't you go too?
                                    (Joyce Johnson)

Another bird agrees:

> We birds have held an honoured place
> Within the annals of your race—
> Elijah's ravens, Noah's dove,
> Leda's swan and Lesbia's love,
> Minerva's owl, Keats' nightingale,
> And Chanticleer in Chaucer's tale.
> Yet on the whole I think that birds
> Should judge you by your deeds not words—
> By scrawny fowls in crowded pen
> Producing cheaper eggs for men,
> By sea-gulls black with oily goo,
> By grouse's August Waterloo,
> By yearly feasts when once again
> All the Innocents are slain—
> And fly away from all save bards
> And spinsters painting Christmas cards.
>
> (O. Banfield)

Parodies of newspaper columnists' Nature Notes, with or without regard to accurate natural history:

No June afternoon feels complete without the sleepy, reiterative tinkle of the copper-throated dimity from its haunt in the hazels: 'Croquet-balls, croquet-balls.' This is the month, too, when to one who is content to wait the orange-blotched nidder—the most resplendent of our native lizards—can be spied darting across the lane. I saw the same female that was here last June. Incredibly the intrepid creature had survived the Arctic rigour and the loss in this very spot of her old mate beneath the non-pneumatic tyres of the rector's iron-framed bicycle which ferries him to and from interments.

(George Moor)

Out in the wilder haunts of the windswept dales—where the young frogwort fidgets whimsically in the quaint old coppices dotting the peaty ground—there is a stirring. One leafy dell sported a pair of vermilion toadfishers, preening themselves like teenagers in the coruscating showers of sun. I was blessed indeed to catch them at full throttle, with their distinctive *quirk-quirk* scandalising the little stream which the rising river tipples from. Summer, claim local folk, continues until Autumn is finished. Be that as it may, the dragonflies are already dancing their hornpipe on the watery rivulets by the lissome willows. Last week, I sighted a badger bagging its first meal of the new season: an indolent chinaworm, its natty new camouflage no comfort. Where else could one breathe such palpitating, passionate air? One must ask the wagtail.

(Belle R. Welling)

The staccato cries of the bar-tailed godwits ring out at sunset as they depart to winter in Timbuktu. The speckled bullfrog utters his last croak before diving to hibernate beneath the imminently freezing pond. Dung beetles are busy collecting mud and straw for their tiny shelters under the rhododendrons. The horn-billed platypus, now well established in the Home Counties, beds down in his snug burrow under the eucalyptus tree. The ghostly hoot of the greater tufted owl echoes at midnight through the leafless glades, where wild donkeys huddle together for warmth in the bitter wind. Now is the time to secure your hen-coops from the assaults of foxes and protect stored potatoes from the ravenous bandicoot. Another winter is come, but life must go on and Spring, though long deferred, will come again.

(Desmond)

Two poems for inclusion in Old Smith's Book of Practical Dogs:

When Scotland Yard is baffled, when Interpol's in doubt,
They always send for Ralph because they know he'll help them
    out,
He never is outwitted by the problems villains pose—
There's nothing hid from Ralph the celebrated Private Nose.

He seems to know of every crime before it can occur,
'Twas he got Fingers Guntle given twenty years in stir;
He nabbed the Upper Clatford Set red-handed on the job,
Exposed the Maulvis Gang and then broke up the Grotti Mob.
No one can catch him napping for he's always on his toes—
There's nothing hid from Ralph the celebrated Private Nose.

Then when you see him strolling so benignly in the Square,
Don't imagine for a moment he's just there to take the air,
Or think he's only idling or admiring of the view,
Make no mistake, just watch your step; he'll have his eye on you,
And all your guilty secrets he could sniff out if he chose—
There's nothing hid from Ralph the celebrated Private Nose.
(Richard Probyn)

McQuiddity, McQuiddity, there's no one like McQuiddity,
His errors are so vulgar and so coarse in their solidity;
You may walk along the pavement, you may step upon the stair,
It's odorously evident McQuiddity's been there.

McQuiddity, McQuiddity, there's no one like McQuiddity,
He doesn't know the meaning of decorum or timidity;
He barks at friends and neighbours and will give the boss a
    scare,
But when burglars cart the silver off he doesn't turn a hair.
If you stagger through a doorway with an overloaded tray
You can bet that old McQuiddity is lying in the way;
If chocolates vanish overnight, or gloves vacate a chair,
Then it's absolutely certain that McQuiddity's been there . . .

McQuiddity, McQuiddity, there's no one like McQuiddity,
He's totally unrivalled in the depth of his stupidity;
His canine infelicities no cretin could surpass,
And he's undisputed champion of the Disobedience Class.
(Mary Holtby)

In Afric's burning deserts,
Where apes swing to and fro
From cactus bough to cactus bough,
And gibber as they go;

In Nepal's snowy mountains,
Where on each sunlit crag
The yak lifts up his hornèd head
And bellows like a stag;

In depths of dark Pacific,
Where in his coral cave
The squid blows inky bubbles up
Which burst upon each wave;

In strange and foreign places
All beasts, with one accord,
Express in their peculiar way
The wonders of the Lord.
   (Robert Ingham)

In Afric's burning deserts,
 Where apes swing to and fro,
In icy climes where penguins
 Leap o'er the frozen floe,
In Argentine's savannahs,
 Where freely roams the horse,
God gives to all His creatures
 The power to feel remorse.

In far Cathay the panda
    Beside the bamboo-bole,
Th'Antipodean wombat,
    The walrus at the Pole—
Each emulates the peacock
    That opes his beak in Ind
To cry his harsh confession:
    '*Peccavi*, I have sinn'd.'
        (Tony Brode)

Burns addressed a mouse. Here are some sympathetic lines to an ant:

I nearly stept on ye, puir struggling mite,
For tears o'anguish dim my downward sight
And yet—a thinking man might weel be right
    Tae tak' your life,
For you and me, wee ant, we share the plight
    O' endless strife.
We struggle on wi' tasks too great to bear—
Your burden, that I see ye pushin' there,
Is big's my ain—a crushin' toil and care
    (I canna roll it!)
But yet—push on. For though our life is sair
    We baith maun thole it.
        (Dromore)

And to a moth:

With swirling swoop and joyful roll,
Out of the midnight damp,
The moth achieves its simple goal
And joins me round my lamp.

Poor feckless nomad of the night,
Fellow insomniac,
Who flaunts no sting, no venomed bite,
Would I could claim thy lack.

Ah fleeting, fey, nocturnal wraith,
Thy wild ecstatic flight
Doth make me wish for thy blind faith
In searching for the light.
                    (Gerry Hamill)

Which? *applied its grading technique to household pets and placed
tortoises, goldfish, hamsters and gerbils among the low scorers.
Competitors were asked to show their own preferences (or dislikes):*

Enough of this absurd debate!
No other beast can emulate
That Creature of Most High Estate—
    The Cat.

Throughout your feline pilgrimage—
In antic youth, in yawning age—
My cares you lull, my pangs assuage,
    O Cat!

Ra's hierophants were proud to serve
The riddle of your rapt reserve.
(All those who menace you deserve
    The cat.)

Imperial, yet domestic too:
Aloof, caressive, fickle, true;
All moods and manners meet in you,
    O Cat!
                    (Rufus Stone)

How I abominate the race of cats!
Ah, how I yearn to kick 'em in the slats!
My garden, once the home of songbirds' rites,
Is now the purlieu of these parasites
Who rend the silent night with banshee yowls
And shred each other's ears with lustful growls;
Who come from far and o'er my seedlings cruise,
Uproot them, excavating feline loos.

Over this nesting-box, a wren's domain,
Grimaukin drapes himself, a catty Cain;
The frantic parent birds his claws will carve
If they approach, and so the fledglings starve.
That blackbird's nest Tibalt forbears to snatch,
Yet when woodpigeons on my young peas prey,
Maukin and Tibalt look the other way.
(Richard Probyn)

Extracts from biographies of their pets written by two literary figures:

from Rochester's Biographie of His Louse
Hector's birthe was cloked in Mysterie, though 'tis likely he came of a
Noble House, for he attach'd himself to me at a Rout at My Lady
Shrewsbury's, in whose Bedd I awoke. 'Tis true Ide pass'd the
Forenoone in the Stewes, but had remark'd no Bites. The best Blood in
England ran in Hector's Veines, not least Old Rowley's; aye, and the
Pox too, but of that later. He had a sure Nose for a Pritty Woman,
towards whome I would extend a Foote for him to hop up their
petticoates, whence on his Retourne his Nipps would impart the most
fiery Itch. He doated too upon Rhenish, ever supping upon the
Drunkenest in the Companie . . . His End was valiant indeed. Her
Majestie suddenly clapt her Hand to her Placket and brought it away
crying "Faugh! A Louse!" 'Twas Hector, fallen thus gloriously upon
the very Field of Honour.
(Tom Brewer)

Sir Walter Scott

In October 1824 died my most faithful ancient friend and servant, Maida, fidus Achates, the noblest of all dogs that ever shared the fellowship of man. He was a large iron-grey staghound of the breed of Ban and Buscar and in the prime of his days could seize and overthrow the powerful red stag. Of most grave demeanour, he deported himself with dignity and decorum becoming his age and size. The old boy could shake the Eildon hills with his roaring but like the great gun at Constantinople it took him so long to get ready the smaller guns would fire off a dozen times first. He had been sketched so often that he would get up and walk off with signs of loathing whenever he saw an artist unfurl his paper and handle his brushes. Maida. His very name seemed made on purpose to close a hexameter.

(Helen MacGregor)

Sonnets containing a man's address to a fish and the fish's reply:

> 'A common goldfish in a cheap glass bowl,
> A fairground lucky win your purchase-fee,
> Set on a kitchen window-sill, I see
> Your treadmill round, your ever-circling roll.
> A bored compassion gives a meagre dole
> Of packet-food—and water, that is free!
> By all the gods of river, lake and sea,
> I pity you, a prisoner with no soul.'
> The fish made answer—though I heard no sound:
> 'A daily manna for my food descends:
> I do not toil, commute or ply for hire.
> The subtle music of my constant round
> You cannot hear. A shaft of sunlight bends—
> My bowl is golden and my robe is fire!'
>
> (O. Banfield)

> 'When I consider how your life is spent
> In a perpetual sort of aimless glide,

Forever at the mercy of the tide,
Shorn of a shell or natural armament,
I wonder what your Maker could have meant
By making you so prone to piscicide.
Did God create you just to have you fried,
And served as self-denying fare in Lent?'
The humble fish replies: 'I do not need
Man's gift for lying, nor his hairy chest.
I'm a mild joke when lying on a plate,
But given grace and beauty when I speed
Through rivers, lakes and oceans without rest:
They also serve who only undulate.'
                                    (Roger Woddis)

A Bit of Earth

Poems starting, unlike T. E. Brown's famous one, 'A garden is a loathsome thing, God wot!'

A garden is a loathsome thing, God wot!—
A veritable blot
Made up of weed and broken flowerpot,
Squat gnome and blighted apricot,
Trampled forget-me-not,
Rank lily, wasp, inedible shallot.
That geezer should be shot
What wrote that lot
Of Palgrave's Golden Tommy-rot,
That T. E. Brown, he seems to have forgot:
Left to itself a garden goes to pot.
Not that I don't enjoy a neat, well-ordered plot,
A nice secluded spot;
I do, but when it rains it's not
Much cop, and when it's hot
I'd rather sun myself on Uncle's yacht.
                    (Gerard Benson)

A garden is a loathsome thing, God wot!
He walks in mine? Good God, what tommy-rot.
I mowed and sowed and hoed, grew very hot;
A load of unferned grot was all I got.

My stocks of phlox and flocks of stocks
And hollyhocks,
Azaleas and dahlias—
All were failures.

Afflicted with some rare disease,
Ignored by butterflies and bees,
Convolvuluted apple trees
Danced fruitlessly upon the breeze.

The lawn was just a mass of pallid clover.
It's all right now—I've paved the whole lot over.
My hands are rough; I've had enough
Of Godwot Brown and all that stuff.
(I. C. Snell)

On the darker side of Spring:

Equinoxious
Now grows the grass with tiresome speed,
Replete with every kind of weed;
Lumbago makes the gardener creak
And pimples mar the youthful cheek.
The quarter's bills show soaring costs,
The blossom's nipped by April frosts
For, captious as some awful child,
The Spring gives way to tantrums wild
From storms of tears to boisterous play—
Sun, snow and thunder in one day.
In Spring the adolescent young
By Love to verse or worse are stung;
Their parents' peace in Love's clove-hitch
Is menaced by the Seven Year Itch
Till in Spring's yeasty ferment we
Are tossed like flotsam on the sea.

Mid such infernal vernal themes,
Ahead how fair the Summer seems;
In retrospect how heaven-sent
The Winter of our discontent.
                    (Richard Probyn)

The
Moving Finger
Writes

Daisy Ashford continues writing in the next world:

O dear Im afraid Mr Salteena is still awfully mere.

Yesterday he asked St Peter if he new anyone called Ethel. Ethel said St Peter why yes I do believe I saw her talking to an arkangle wearing a frock of mouve velvit yellow gluvs and a beautifull expression.

Thankyou my good fellow said Mr Salteena exyuding bonomy.

Oh said St Peter there was also a tall man of 29 with them.

Was he rarther bent with long legs fairish hair and blue eyes said Mr S.

Yes said St Peter.

Curses said Mr S thats Bernard hes an Athama to me. So he tipped St Peter 2/6 and went to see the Prince of Wales who said hard luck Hyssops wimin are sly foxes and dark horses eh.

(David Phillips)

My aboad is indeed a handsome place with mouve couches and clouds in pink and white. Champaigne and things like that appear like majic and there is lots of peace and quiut and fun if you want it to. I have seen Saynt Peter and spoke to him reveruntly asking him if he would have a glass of champaigne. He grasusly accepted. One grows weary Cherrybims he remarked, lapping up his rasberry ice.

Well now I must go out now and call on a few anjels, said Saynt Peter picking up his elegent hello.

Adiue my Lord I cried. We meet anon I take it.

Not till tomorrow answered Saynt Peter at the Holey Spirits place at 4 where you will no doubt find tea.

(T. Griffiths)

Oscar Wilde deigns to speak to a medium:

M: What do you think of Eternity so far?
O: It is a greater disappointment than Niagara Falls. There is only one thing more tedious than Eternity and that is Infinity. Here one gets a plethora of both.
M: Surely it is very scenically exciting?
O: The vistas are unvaryingly bland, like dining for ever on steamed veal, and the company is unbearably vulgar.
M: Are you allowed to tell us whether you are in Heaven or Hell?
O: I am, but I have no intention of satisfying your curiosity. Suffice it to say that it is uncannily similar to Pall Mall.
M: Are people in the spirit world happy?
O: One finds innumerable spirits crying out to be laid, but it seems that there is very little that one can do to help them.
M: Have you any message for anybody here in the corporeal world?
O: Yes. Warn Alfie that Hell is bottomless.

(Gerard Benson)

M: . . . er . . . may I speak to you, Mr Wilde? Have you any advice for us?
O: You may listen while I relay through you a little unwordly wisdom. Attend carefully, because the morality of art consists in the perfect use of an imperfect medium. The two defects of your age are its want of principle and its want of profile: Prohibition and the Charleston are responsible for both. You destroy Art and have made an art of destruction; pleasure you have made your business so that idleness becomes your burden. You have fought a war against those respectable Germans, and you will fight another. What advice can *I* give you?
M: I shall repeat your every word.
O: Rien ne change.

(J. C. Causer)

Lady Jane Grey comments on the Tower of London's 900th anniversary:

Tell the centuries, mighty Tower.
I who go my vasty ways
from sixteen years to nine days
outlast your hour—
the bones that crack within your walls,
the blood-red rust that wracks your cup,
the bridegroom's head held lustily up
after the axe falls,
the winter white upon your green
where ravens cry above dry crowns
like dusty scholars in black gowns
fighting about a queen . . .
yes, I have seen you long ago—
an old cold dark Tower
that in the moment of its power
was blotted out by snow.

(Gina Berkeley)

A tragic hero and a tragic heroine cope with everyday matters:

To shave, or not to shave: that is the question:
Whether 'tis easier on the chin to suffer
The pricks and stubble of an evening shadow,
Or to take soap against a field of stubble,
And by a razor end it? To soap, to shave;
No more: and by a shave to say we end
The shadow and the thousand prickly points
That chins are heir to, 'tis a consummation
Devoutly to be wished. To soap, to shave,
To shave; perchance to nick: ay, there's the rub;
For in that sea of foam what nicks may come
When we have lathered all the shrinking chin,
Must give us pause. There's the respect

That makes calamity of a morning shave,
For who would risk a stinging, painful nick,
When he might save himself the trouble daily
With a handsome beard? Who would shaving bear,
To smart and grimace under tickling foam,
But that the dread of breadcrumbs, clinging egg,
Doth make us rather shave, come morn again . . .
(T. Griffiths)

(Hedda is in kitchen. Enter Tesman, her husband.)

TESMAN: Hedda—my dearest—how is this? *You* peeling potatoes!

HEDDA: Cook has deserted us.

TESMAN: Deserted—?

HEDDA: A ship berthed in the harbour, and she's run off with one of the sailors. A long-lost lover, apparently.

TESMAN: What infamy, what—!

HEDDA: Fortune has beamed on her. She has escaped into the illimitable richness of the world.

TESMAN: Hedda—!

HEDDA: And I am shackled to this knife, in this domestic prison cell, shaving potatoes.

TESMAN (*surveying her work*): How wonderfully you are doing it, my dear Hedda! (*Peering closer*) But, if I may be permitted to advise, surely you must cut out those eyes, so-called.

HEDDA (*fiercely*): You ask me *that*?

TESMAN: Well—

HEDDA (*wildly*): To root out the sproutings, callously to destroy some future flowering of life . . . To become the squalid abortionist of the grandeur of creation!
(John Digby)

A Dickens novel summarised in three limericks:

Nicholas Nickleby

At Dotheboys Hall, Nick's a teacher,
It's ghastly, but matters soon reach a
   Head, and (three cheers!)
   Nick thrashes old Squeers,
And clears off with Smike, the poor creature.

Uncle Ralph, wicked brother of Daddy's,
Gets mad when the chivalrous lad is
   In time to save Kate
   From a terrible fate,
For all of Ralph's buddies are baddies.

Kate watches Smike die, rather tearfully,
And Ralph, being found out so fearfully,
   Commits suicide,
   And the murder of Gride
Makes everything end very cheerfully.
           (A. J. Wyborn)

Poems which Dr Spooner might have composed:

When from tempting scenes I hide me,
   Musing in my *cheesy air*,
Then I have a *bower* with *Onion*,
   Or I *muddy Stilton* there.

As a *grim pill* I would travel
   With companions such as these,
With them, *glad* in *codlike* wisdom,
   My own mind I *ooze* to *cheese*.
           (Joyce Johnson)

In my *dung yeas*, while still a boy,
Word-botching was my only joy.
Why! Even *oaring beagles* could
Create for me a *mappy hood*!

An ardent con*ver*sationist,
No *beery word* I ever missed,
And often saved, *scrawled* by a *quiche*,
Pale muffins stranded on the beach.

Now that I'm old, and *growing gay*,
I cannot *brace turds* every day,
But none the less *tan cake* delight
In watching *bumming herds* in flight.
(Peter Peterson)

Sweet *Hairy Muse*, my *paltering fashion* speaks.
Soap in my *hole*, my *qualm*, my *bean*,
Your *haven rare* and ruddy *chips* and *leeks*
Remind me of *my Anna's dean*.

O *greasy bodice* of the *darkling spawn*,
Please *clip* me *gross* to your *braced chest*,
That I may lie there like a *fetid pawn*
And in a peaceful *riot quest*.
(Larry Hime)

Wodehouse and Kafka change places:

Blandings Castle *by Franz Kafka* . . .

'I have heard that there is a child from the city here,' said Constance, 'who may not understand, indeed, probably has no idea of, our ways. I therefore consider it prudent to warn her.' 'Warn her?' queried Emsworth. 'I do not care for your tone, Constance, this is no district-visiting occasion.' 'You mean?' Emsworth drew himself up to

(33)

his not inconsiderable height and gazed blearily blue-eyed down at his sister. The fact that his pince-nez were slightly askew did nothing to rob him of his dignity. In an odd way they served to enhance it, giving him the air of one who was above having to adjust such small details in order to emphasise his position. 'You understand quite well, I think', he replied, 'that I will not countenance any word or action that would tend to give this resourceful and gallant young lady cause for embarrassment.'

(A. J. Wyborn)

. . . and The Castle *by P. G. Wodehouse*

K. could see no glimmer of light in the situation. The Castle looked little better than a piece of ribbon development that had gone wrong, and a fat lot of good that was from the sightseeing point of view, so he toddled up to a cottage and heaved a snowball at a window.

'Well?' enquired a man with a beard not dissimilar in size or texture to a Nepalese prayer mat.

'I'd be awfully obliged if you could let me have a bit of sit-down,' K. said soothingly, giving him the old oil. 'I'm the new land surveyor, don't you know.'

'Rrr . . .' breathed the old man through lips that, like the Windmill, never closed.

K. trickled in and sank into a chair.

'You can't stay here,' boomed a second man, with a smaller beard, resembling a startled hedgehog.

'Absolutely not!' K. assured him. 'Just a spot of rest, what?'

(T. Griffiths)

Competitors were invited to describe a person by a list of twenty-six adjectives beginning with the letters of the alphabet taken in order:

Sir Alf Ramsey

Adamantine, bland, calm, detached, enigmatic, forceful, gentlemanly, hardhearted, individualistic, judicious, knightly, loyal, modest,

Napoleonic, obstinate, persistent, quiet, resolute, sardonic, taciturn, unflappable, vigilant, wilful, exacting, yogic, zealous.

(R. W. Dargavel)

Edward Heath

Abrasive, bloody-minded, cussed, disposable, Elgar-conducting, frosty, grimacing, hawkish, imperious, juggernautish, keen, middle-class, natty, organ-playing, platitudinous, quick-tempered, ruthless, semi-French-speaking, tactless, unmarried, vain, worried, ex-conservative, yacht-besotted, zigzagging.

(E. O. Parrott)

Edward Lear

Avuncular, bearded, chubbly, diligent, entertaining, fastidious, grumbly, hoddy-doddy, illustratious, Jumbly-loving, kindly, lachry-mose, myopic, nonsensical, original, pleasant, queer, runcible-hatted, spherical, topographical, unprepossessing ('His visage is more or less hideous'), versed, white-waterproofed ('He walks in a waterproof white'), extravagantly-syllabled (e.g. 'splendidophoropherostipphon-gious'), Yonghy-Bonghy-Bo-ian, zoographical.

(Amy Johnson)

A retelling of Chaucer:

The Knight's Tale (P. G. Wodehouse)

'Jeeves,' I said, 'I have an amazing tale to relate.'

'Indeed sir?'

'Yes Jeeves. Old "Thicky" Theseus is back from Scythia and now domiciled in Steeple Bumpleigh with the frightful rhinoceros woman.'

'Hippolyta, sir.'

'Hippolyta, yes. He also has in tow Emilia, sister of above. Well, the other night, Thicky stormed into the Drones, lays out old Creon and hauls home those two perfectly sound eggs Palamon and Arcite. And mark the sequel, Jeeves.'

'I am agog, sir.'

'The dynamic duo both fall in love with Emilia, having heard her warbling in the gardens and messuages. Arcite is handed the mitten, so he pronto changes his name to Pentheo and hotfoots it to Mycenae to work as butler to a bimbo called, if I have the name right, Menelaus.'

Jeeves allowed an eyebrow to rise an eighth of an inch.

'Most disturbing, sir,' he said.

(Barry Knowles)

Extracts from two sub-Wildean plays and one sub-Cowardly scenario in which the characters strain to be epigrammatically witty to ghastly effect:

(Scene: Lord Sidewinder's gun-room. Enter *Lord Sidewinder* and *Hargreaves* the gamekeeper.)

Lord S: Game's pretty thin this year, Hargreaves.

Hargreaves: Her Ladyship insists that Lent is strictly observed in the coverts, my Lord.

Lord S: Eh?

(Enter *Ronald*, Lord Sidewinder's son.)

Lord S: Ah, Ronald, I hear you've been sent down. Disgraceful!

Ronald: Oxford is like the train to Didcot. One is never certain where one will alight, due to the state of the track.

(Enter *Celia*.)

Ronald (Wearily): Kissing one's sister is rather like looking at Duchamp's Mona Lisa—one wonders whether the moustache might not be dispensed with.

(*Celia* weeps.)

Hargreaves: Bear up, Miss, remember sisterly affection is like a butler watering the port, best kept within reasonable limits.

(Gong sounds.)

Lord S: Good-oh, grub up.

(They go in.)

Hargreaves: When the Last Trump sounds for the Upper Class it will be sounded on a dinner gong, as like as not.

(J. Dean)

(The rockery at Muldoons. *Charles* is at work with a small garden fork. Enter *Gerald*.)
Gerald: Weeding, Charles?
Charles: Dear weeds, so like us: we're weedy, and wish we weren't; they're weeded, and wish *they* weren't! (Enter *Mrs Waventry* in black.) Here comes a woman with a past!
Gerald: Their pasts are so often our futures.
Charles: And whenever we invest in them, they slump! Have *you* ever invested, Mrs Waventry?
Mrs Waventry: No: only *di*vested! We women have but one commodity.
Gerald: And yours was—unsound?
Mrs Waventry: Never: for it has won me—my weeds!
(Exeunt *Gerald*, *Mrs Waventry*, and *Charles*, arms round each other's waists, laughing hysterically.)
(Roger Jeffreys)

Tristan: . . . but, Laetitia, there is absolutely no point in being naïve. The naïve are invariably praised for being inordinately clever.
Laetitia: True. But every genius I meet is simple-minded.
Tristan: My dear, geniuses work so terribly hard. That is why they are simple: mental exercise is thoroughly brainless.
Laetitia: I expect that's why most scientists are bachelors: husbands are frightfully clever.
Tristan: That is why they are so frightful. I devote our marriage to being frightful.
Laetitia: But you never seem frightful!
Tristan: Only because you are naïve. If there's one thing worse than being naïve, it's being very naïve.
Laetitia: I do not follow.
Tristan: That is because you are naïve.
(Ellen Brigwell)

Nothing to Eat
but Food

Menus for a sick-making anti-Lucullan feast presented the following delicacies:

Mint Bloater Soup
Donkey Liver Mousse, Butterscotch Sauce
Sow's Udders in Aspic with Whelk Fritters
Liquorice Potatoes, Crystallised Sprouts
Parsnip Porridge
Goat's Kidneys in Marmalade
Camembert and Rhubarb Waffles
Sardine Shortbread
Mentholated Coffee
(Gerry Hamill)

Hors d'Oeuvre Maison
Whelks, Pontefract cakes, boiled liver and fresh ants' eggs in a chilled purée of swede

Baleine à l'Ecossaise
Whale brains in whisky sauce

Porc Tartare
Served with roast banana skins, pickled fudge and crushed Horlicks tablets

Coupe Royale
Tomato ice-cream topped with anchovies, garlic, tea-leaves, salted peanuts and crème de menthe

Café Minceur
A blend of coffee, alcohol-free lager and carrot juice

Bon-bons Surprise
Chocolate-covered oysters
                    (Basil Ransome-Davies)

Hilaire Belloc once wrote a sonnet beginning 'Would that I had £300,000.' Competitors were invited to indulge their fantasies and compose their own sonnets to Mammon:

These I have loved:
   White pearls and diamonds gleaming,
Rings with blue sapphires, bracelets wrought in gold;
The lustre of wild silk, and sunlight streaming
On silver vases, orchid-filled; the old
Soft colours of fine porcelain; the taste
Of vintage port, the sparkle of champagne;
Smoked salmon, caviare and peaches laced
With brandy; then, the perfumes that remain
Aloof from fashion's dictates (Worth, Chanel),
Ball gowns by Dior for the festive nights
In Paris; Rolls-Royce cars . . . Why, I could tell
Of a thousand other pleasures and delights . . .
I have been so great a lover; my heart sings
Its praise for Mammon's rich, expensive things.
                    (Mary C. Kellock)

Give me the mundane pleasures of the flesh,
The roast of sirloin and the Yorkshire pud
With petits-pois and cauliflower afresh,
And lashings of the crisp and golden spud.
Now let the rich brown gravy gently lap
The dab of yellow mustard on the side,
Decant that fruity Châteauneuf-du-Pape,
Which, wed to beef, doth make the perfect bride,

And crowns the very peak of my delight.
Those who would spurn the riches of the earth
—The fasting monk, or spartan anchorite,
With haggard visage and a wasted girth—
Are simply demonstrating that they can
Despise sweet Heaven's gifts to mortal man.
(Gerry Hamill)

A poem, in the style of Ogden Nash, on a cocktail party:

There are all kinds of parties, but the kind I
    don't like are
Those where the host is a piker—

The kind of guy who puts you on rations,
Like a handful of pecans, four canapés, and two
　　Old Fashioneds—
And where, instead of dancing the rhumba
With a cute little number,
You end up heartbroken
On a sofa with some little old lady from
　　Hoboken,
Usually a Seventh Day Adventist,
Who son is—guess what?—a dentist.
I don't know what's worse—hearing about the jerk's
　　enviable salary
Or surviving all evening on about half a calorie.
　　　　　　(Basil Ransome-Davies)

Pin up
Your Hair with All
Your Letters

Embarrassing letters accompanying literary offerings, from three hopeful authors to their prospective publishers:

May I say at once, I do not aim at the financial rewards of best-selling popularity—a view of literature which your recent catalogue suggest you share. That being so, I send the MS of my book, *Heavenly Moments*. I believe *ars est celare artem*; maybe you will agree that mine is well concealed. I may add that I was encouraged to submit my work by a Mr Trowner, himself an author, though unpublished for psychosomatic reasons. I have not enclosed stamps for return as I have been professionally advised to resist rejection.

(Edward Samson)

I am sure your reader will give to the MS of my novel (herewith) the attention it deserves. However, since it employs some rather unusual devices, I have thought fit to offer him/her some guidance.

The action—which I prefer to call the *évènements*—takes place on three (3) levels, viz: the realistic (individual), the symbolic (universal), and the ritualistic (sociological). The characters, or *personae*, are deliberately undifferentiated. The narrator is at times the author; at other times the hero/anti-hero narrates, and sometimes a disembodied voice, which can be taken variously as destiny, the chorus, or the creative principle itself, takes over.

With regard to the format, I had thought a kind of scroll, on the principle of the ancient Roman and Jewish books, might seem appropriate. Reduced to its simplest form, the book would then have an appearance not dissimilar to a roll of toilet paper.

(David Wilson)

The rather large (!!) parcel that comes with this letter is my thought poem, *My Friends the Trees*. I know you will be interested in it because you are a Sagittarius. It is written on a special paper made from rabbits' doings that is my own invention because trees do not like to be made into paper but rabbit doings do not mind. I know this because the trees told me. My poem, which is my own story, tells more what the trees said to me and I have made it so each different coloured ink SIGNIFIES a different sort of tree; for instance, orange is an orange tree. All but the last 1,000 pages I did in SECRET WRITING so CERTAIN PEOPLE could not read it. Please send the money in postal orders or THEY will steal it. I must warn you BAD LUCK COMES TO HIM who disobeys the trees.

(Balthazar Ngaga)

Two publishers write letters of rejection for the Book of Genesis:

Sir: Now concerning the things whereof you wrote (a) even the First Book of Moses called GENESIS, thus saith the Lord, (b) publish it not (c) As it is written (d), thou art weighed in the balance and found wanting (e); it is a foolish thing to make a long prologue and to be short in the story itself (f) You see how large a letter I have written unto you (g); blessed is he that readeth (h). This is the way (j); let it be written (k) with ink and pen (l) with your own hands (m), comprehending much in few words (n); neither give heed to fables and endless genealogies (o). Though I made you sorry with a letter, I do not repent (p), and further, by these, my son, be admonished (q); write the vision, and make it plain, that he may run that readeth (r). Wherefore I desire that you faint not (s); of making many books there is no end (t).

[Sources: (a) 1 Cor.7.1 (b) Isa.66.1. (c) 2 Sam.1.20. (d) Rom.4.17. (e) Dan.5.27. (f) Macc.2.32. (g) Gal.6.11. (h) Rev.1.3 (j) Isa.30.21. (k) Esth.1.19. (l) John.3.13. (m) 1 Thess.4.11 (n) Ecclus.32.8. (o) 1 Tim.1.4. (p) 2 Cor.7.8. (q) Ecc.12.12. (r) Hab.2.2. (s) Eph.3.13. (t) Ecc.12.12.]

(Tom Brewer)

Sir: We thank you for submitting your manuscript for our consideration.

In his report our Reader writes that he finds your book unusual and highly original and that he cannot remember ever having come across a work of more powerful imagination. From the account of the creation of the world, the strange sequence of the various living things and the charming story of the Garden of Eden until its tragic end, through to the death of the great character you call Joseph, the book covers a most impressive span of human activity. However, he finds the book in some respects rather confused, with some duplication of incidents and references to the same character under different names which give the impression of inadequate revision. Furthermore, many of the book's incidents are too fantastic to be acceptable to our readers. We therefore regretfully return it herewith.

Yours faithfully,
The Tabernacle Press
(H. A. C. Evans)

Two shrewdly revealing references intended to enlighten a student's prospective landlady:

This is to introduce my neighbour's son, Ivor Bannerman, who I am pleased to say will shortly be leaving home to become a student at Oxford. Ivor is obviously a popular young man as is indicated by the many friends he entertains in his room adjoining mine, and he will easily conform to the student pattern. He is a person of principle, and prepared to go to any lengths, however uncomfortable or painful, to demonstrate the strength of his convictions. As an older man I do not know the names of all his sparetime pursuits, but I am well acquainted with his records of modern music which, if you accept him, I hope all your other guests will be able to enjoy. His car is somewhat old, but he works on it enthusiastically and would drive you anywhere with it. I am glad to help Ivor along his chosen road.

(Stuart Woods)

I have known Mr — for longer than I care to remember; for he lodged with us whilst working at the skin-yard and in his first years at College. He brought into our house something which will never completely fade.

He is economical and never one to linger in the bathroom to the detriment of others, neither does he spend recklessly on outer clothing and personal linen. He is popular within a small circle of friends of either sex who are in and out of his quarters with great good fellowship, although motorcycle spare-parts and accoutrements leave little room for entertaining.

Generous by nature, on occasion he has asked us out for a drink and, unlike so many young people today, he was never too proud to let us 'do the honours'. Likewise his farewell party, an unforgettable occurrence.

(Michael Birt)

A devastating letter couched in dreadful good humour to an injured swain:

Dear Michael, Must thank you for a *great* party last night—*really* good music with just the right number of 'smoochies'! Caroline's a good dancer, isn't she? Actually, while I'm on Caroline (*sorry*, no pun intended) I feel I should apologise for what happened. I expect you're upset (and surprised?) but I honestly had *no* idea that Caroline was your fiancée—nobody in the Regiment had. (Somehow we just never thought of *Caroline* having a 'steady'—I don't know why.) Still, *good news*—now they know, one or two chaps feel they owe you a drink at least—should be quite a binge! Anyway, I feel awful; I wish it could have been anyone else but me you'd found. Please forgive me.

Yours,
Edward.

P.S. Caroline says she forgot her engagement ring last night and could you bring it over? It's probably in the ashtray by your bed. *Thanks*.

(John C. H. Mounsey)

Thank-you letters after an appalling country weekend which half-consciously convey a feeling quite other than gratitude:

Dear Gran, I hope you are well. I am quite well, thank you. Thank you for the lovely weekend. It must be funny for you having no telly. I read in a book how people used to make their own entertainment but perhaps this wasn't your weekend for making entertainment. Do you always go to church twice on Sundays? Mum says she'll never forget Sundays when she was a girl. She says you always used to have milk pudding for lunch too and then cold at supper-time like we did. She never ever makes milk pudding now.

I'm awfully sorry about that old cup I broke and I'm sure the clock will be OK. I'd nearly got it mended when you came in. I think I left a submarine in the goldfish pond. Can you post it please? But I must stop now. With love from George.

(G. H. Harris)

Sorry late writing. Tummy trouble, I'm afraid—a tribute to your cook's rich offerings!

Thank you for a unique weekend. I cannot remember one like it, both for the welcome and company. One felt one had fallen among characters in a novel, presided over by your genius for hospitality, not easily forgotten. So often today guests are left alone, but you organised so many games and activities one felt spoilt.

Alas! It may be long before I shall see your lovely house again, since I am going far away; but the memory will not fade, believe me.

P.S. If a Rolex Oyster Perpetual turns up, it's mine! Possibly mislaid hurrying to catch the train. Do keep the electric razor and gold cuff-links, if found. Cheque book and credit cards all safely cancelled. My wretched carelessness. These things are sent to try us, aren't they?

(T. Griffiths)

Darling Mags, I should have done this long ago but since leaving you I have been wondering whether your fabulous weekend really happened. What an ice-breaker that badger hunt was on our first evening—and then charades to warm us up. After all that rain on Saturday a punt pub-crawl was an inspiration. So silly of us to jam in the reeds though—but then you did say the pub was packed out anyway. And what a coincidence Serge and Zloty having the same birthday. Such fun to taste Slav civilisation at first hand—and that slivovitz! So clever of you to introduce a Russian tang to everything. Where *did* you hear of seagull soup? I'll send you some of that Spanish tummy remedy I promised as soon as I'm out again.

(Peggy Sandars)

Shakespeare
Was One of Us

A poem in which each line's rhymed ending is a truncated word:

Supposing that the Bard of Av.
Had caught this hab. and written *Ham.*,
Would he be held in so much fav.?
Would he be called the greatest dram.?
For who could stomach Ob. and Tit.?
Or Ant. and Cle.? Would Rome. and Ju.
Sound quite as trag.? Could one feel pit.
Or horror at the Rape of Lu.?
And to abbrev. Sir John to Fal.
Would hardly please his Pist. and Bard.;
And could a Ros. fall for an Orl.
In something called the For. of Ard.?
What's in a name? Much, I conject.
Illyria—had this been Ill.,
Lysander Lys., or Hector Hect.,
Then no great Shakes., perhaps, our Will.
(A. J. Wyborn)

Hamlet *summarised in three limericks:*

Prince Hamlet went nearly insane;
He'd a notable brain for a Dane,
But it muddled his head
When his dad, who was dead,
Told him not to trust Uncle again.

(48)

'I'm only a thinker!' he cried,
'And I always stand by on the side.'
   But by means of a play
   And some spiked Beaujolais
He had his revenge, and he died.

He said to a friend as he fell,
'Stay alive, and be certain to tell
   How I killed off my mother,
   My late father's brother,
And one or two others as well.'
          (Paul Griffin)

An earnest, trendy director explains why he has set a Shakespeare play in a daringly untraditional time and place:

. . . when Kent calls Oswald 'a base football-player', he articulates the quintessential metaphoric relevance of *Lear* to our contemporary culture. The Wembley setting dictates itself; it is mandatory. For here, in this universal world, the possibles play the probables in a floodlit arena, savagely scything each other down, carving up midfields. There are, so to speak, no shin-pads in *Lear*. Cornwall: dismissed at half-time after professionally fouling Gloucester. The Fool: substituted after some dazzling ball-play so that Cordelia can come on. Edgar: playing all over the park, ultimately the sweeper, Shakespeare's Bobby Moore. Meanwhile, the godly referees: trusted too foolishly by all, intervening in too haphazard a fashion. It will be clear from frequent changes of strip how play—the play—develops. The symbolic hanging of Cordelia from the opposition goalpost is surely the only apposite image for this timeless drama of violence.
          (Ellen Brigwell)

Three mock-Shakespearian speeches containing at least ten titles which owe nothing to Shakespeare:

(*Enter* LORD HOWARD)
Lord Jim! I haste, *summoned by bells, the chimes*
A tocsin from *the towers of Trebizond*
Wherein *a group of noble dames, kidnapped*
By *Kim, the warden,* once *our mutual friend,*
Lie chained, for he denies *the rights of man.*
These are *hard times* in truth when *wives and daughters,*
The well-beloved friends of *Princess Ida,*
Are treated thus. *The Countess Cathleen, she*
Whose riches near surpass *the wealth of nations,*
Requires the aid of *sons and lovers,* all
Stout *men-at-arms* and *soldiers. Three* days hence
Shall we assault *the castle,* so withdraw
The *sword of honour* and prepare for war.
If victory may not our cause attend,
Then mortal *strife* shall bring Lord *Howard's end.*
(John Sweetman)

LEAR: Send *the man within.* No room for *fathers?*
And children give a *dusty answer?* No,
Not all her *pride and prejudice* hold back
My firm intent to enter this *bleak house.*
Have I forsworn *the corridors of power*
But to deny my *old mortality*
A place to rest? *Black mischief* in her eyes,
The *wuthering heights* of her rash choler soar
High o'er *the eagle's nest,* I'll not be prey,
Nor list me in *the acceptance world*
Where kings are bondmen. *Crime and punishment*
Go hand in hand: her crime to spurn, her fee
To house *the naked and the dead,* should I
Demand it, *night and day.* Come, my good fool!
(Laurence Fowler)

(Claudius has received a letter chiding him for his lack of ambition.)

CLAUDIUS: *I, Claudius,* would go *where eagles dare,*
Where *kingfishers catch fire,* and *the wild duck,*
The trumpet-major of *the golden bough,*
Summons *the birds* to *larkrise* and the day.
Lord of the rings I'd be, of Jupiter
And Mars, *forever amber*; of the spheres
Whose music fills *the arches of the years*
Making *the universe around us* rich with song,
For O *my son, my son! fame is the spur*
That pricks me on *to kill a mocking-bird*
That jeers within, '*Claudius the god, the moon
Is a balloon! Venus observed* is trash!
The birds fall down to quill an imperial pen
Which scarce could write a *requiem for a wren!*'
Lord of the flies shall I no longer be
—But Livia calls for *tea and sympathy.*
(M. Fanning)

Anagrams of Shakespearian Sonnet lines:

Shall I compare thee to a summer's day?
Hurrah! See, my mice tootle a sad psalm.
(Frances Rhodes)

Love's not Time's fool, though rosy lips and cheeks:
Shun Peter O'Toole's Scots king. Lovely dish of ham.
(E. S. Goodwill)

Thy bosom is endearèd with all hearts:
So end there, silly bastard whom I hate.
(Moyra Blyth)

And sweets grown common lose their dear delight:
'Soldiers rot,' comments the lewd and ageing whore.
(Michael Pickering)

Weary with toil I haste me to my bed:
The bloody time, it withers me away.
(N. E. Soret)

My glass shall not persuade me I am old:
Shampoo me, lass, I'm slate-grey and dull.
(N. E. Soret)

Rough winds do shake the darling buds of May:
Ugh! Weather dismal. No fun had by kids or dogs.
(N. E. Soret)

Shall I compare thee to a summer's day?
My mate's a callous Hermes-Aphrodite.
(Paul Griffin)

Shall I compare thee to a summer's day?
The precious heat a small sad memory.
(B. P. Hall)

Sweet love, renew thy force; be it not said
We hye to toilets 'cos we never fart in bed.
(W. S. Brownlie)

Full many a glorious morning have I seen:
Verily a fine hol, in a summer sun long ago.
(Brocky)

Let not my love be called idolatry:
Cold lady, lovely bitter lemon tea!
(Ellen Brigwell)

Horribly Bored

Three poems, leadenly prosaic in style and content:

> To turn now to your second question, well,
> The basic situation is the same:
> Little has changed; and only time will tell
> If progress has been made except in name.
>
> In my own view—though far be it from me
> To make conjectures in advance of facts—
> It all depends on how the two sides see
> The present issues, and how each side acts.
>
> To some, the view looks good; to others, bad;
> Discussions, hopefully, are under way;
> There really is not much that I can add
> To what was said in statements yesterday.
>
> According to a reputable source,
> More details will be issued in due course.
> (Bridget Loney)

The stations of the London Underground
Are useful points for boarding subway trains.
Extremely numerous, they can be found
By passengers who learn to use their brains.
Infallibly revealed by special signs
(Look out for circles with a transverse bar),

They give the traveller a choice of lines.
Their platform maps will show you where you are.
The tickets, though expensive, are quite small,
Oblong in shape and often coloured green:
They can be purchased in the booking-hall
From booking-clerks, or else from a machine.
The average speed is reasonably fast,
But jolts are harmless if you grip the strap;
And when your destination's reached at last
You safely can descend—but mind the gap.
(Basil Ransome-Davies)

When you are made miserable by the cold wintry blast
In places as widely apart as Toronto, Moscow and Belfast,
You must remember that in three or four months' time
A higher temperature will ensure a reasonably tolerable clime.
Nevertheless, nobody but God can foretell the precise date
When the unpredictable winter will finally abate,
Thus bringing to all and sundry the much desired spring
About which ninety per cent of poets and birds sing.
(Robert Greacen)

Monologues by some Great Bores:

. . . and here's the hotel steps again. That's a Mrs Wilkins. Or was it
Wilson? No, Watkins. And he's a man called George with a banana on
his head. He was a real scream. And the window of our room is five
along from the one behind George's head. And that's all of us going on
a coach trip, only Jim had his thumb in the way, so you can only see
our feet, which is a pity as George had a stick of rock behind his ear.
And those feet belong to a very nice lady whose son had an interesting
job in insurance at Clapham. Or was it Clacton? And this should have
been one of George's dog, only he ran away, but you can see its tail.
I'm so glad you're enjoying these as we've got them going back to
1960 . . .
(B. Mooring)

. . . oh really? yes well Katie asks to go to the lavatory now and once we've put her down at about six she sleeps through till seven which means that part's quite relaxing now d'you know when Mummy came over the other day she tried to put Katie's duffel coat on her and she said no Katie do it because I've taught her to do the toggles up herself and when I was paying the milkman yesterday she said milk milk she's obviously picked that up in the last week oh did you? America and Mexico? How nice well when David comes home from work she runs and gets Heffalump and Paddington and she . . .

(John Thrower)

. . . of course Placido was telling me at lunch yesterday—gin and tonic everyone?—that he has to limit himself to ten *Otellos* perhaps one should say *Otelli* a year because the part is simply so demanding on the voice I must say I think he's making a marvellous job of it though he hasn't got the sheer power for the big outbursts have you ever heard that wonderful old recording of Martinelli singing *Niun mi tema*? Kleiber's a tremendous asset of course I can't remember when I've ever heard the strings play so well sheer whipped cream and Sachertorte VPO look to your laurels I met Bill Mann in the gents and from what he was saying I think there's bound to be a rave in the *Times* how about going round to see Placido and Margaret afterwards? Birgit darling *how* are you? I'm coming for your next Isolde . . .

(Martin Dickson)

. . . yes, a home delivery is great, I can't describe it as anything else. The midwife was *really* nice, Adrian was *fantastic*, there were *no* hassles at all, except the gasman called in the middle! It was *so nice* being in my own bed and my own nightie. The midwife, she was just like Auntie Joan to look at without the glasses, said I was really good and kept my cool brilliantly considering what a big head Tristram has. You really should have one. Adrian had nothing but praise. He was doubtful beforehand but now he tells all his colleagues how splendid it is and tries to persuade them. And he's very proud of me and keeps giving them *all* the gory details, I don't know how I'll face them when I meet them again . . .

(Mary Smith)

Definitions illustrating the different qualities belonging respectively to a 'nurd', a 'berk', a 'clot', a 'twit' and a 'charlie':

> A *nurd* puts his shoes on before his trousers.
> A *berk* puts his on before his socks.
> A *clot* arouses the head waiter's anger.
> A *twit* arouses his pity.
> A *charlie* does both, and leaves a large tip.
> (I. C. Snell)

A *nurd* is one who sets magazine problems.
A *berk* is a person who attempts to answer such problems.
A *clot* thinks he doesn't have the brains to answer them.
A *twit* forgets to post his entry, and
a *charlie* writes his own address on the envelope.
(K. Otway)

A *nurd* believes everything he reads in the papers.
A *clot* believes everything he reads in the papers except the bits he doesn't agree with.
A *twit* writes for the papers and thinks everyone believes everything he writes.
A *charlie* doesn't trust newspapers. He watches television instead.
(V. Ernest Cox)

Nurd: A media personality whose private life is exposed week after week in the gossip columns thanks to information anonymously supplied by himself.
(G. E. Smith)

Originally a superfluous concretion in the flesh, and, by analogy, a superfluous person. In Lincolnshire one who falls into a ditch without his absence being noted.
(Edgar Lythe)

Berk: Muddied oaf. From S. Lancs dialect 'doun b'Irk', a tributary of the River Irwell in Manchester, where mudlarks used to scavenge in the 19th century.

(Ron Jowker)

An upper-class nurd (*q.v.*). Erroneously associated with Bishop Berkeley of Cloyne, a philosopher who could not believe his eyes.
(Edgar Lythe)

Twit: One who joins the clientele of a marriage bureau and ends up proposing to his ex-wife.

(Frances Rhodes)

Charlie: A person who is not only absent-minded but also absent in body-sense, spirit etc., tending to refer to himself in the third person as 'one'.

(Gerard Benson)

Originally a night-watchmen; an inefficient, forceless person having difficulty even with his brazier. The thought behind the expression 'a proper charlie' is obscure. (W. S. Brownlie)

A chap who will come some day.

(Cecily Croke)

A slow-coach, hence bad driver. Derived from the French *char-au-lait* (milk-float).

(Ron Jowker)

Two poems to suit Tennyson's title for one of his: 'Supposed Confessions of a Sensitive Second-Rate Mind Not in Unity with Itself':

> I sit and think, I think, therefore I am,
> Therefore, I think, I am because I think,
> And then I think my thoughts are all a sham,
> For all the thoughts I think rely on drink.

Sometimes I think, I drink, therefore I am,
Establishing 'twixt dram and am a link,
Which means, I am because I drink—
   oh damn!
I find it hard to think without a drink.

I here confess my mind is second-rate
Until the spirit clarifies my brain,
And then the sober self I do negate.
I think I'm mad to think drink keeps me sane.
        (V. Ernest Cox)

    The woof, it seems, is split,
Likewise the weft; I am bereft
    Mayhap of native wit.

    I cannot hold the thread;
The weave, I say, ever gives way;
    I might as well be dead.

    And yet time was when I
Went not far wrong, plodded along
    Somewhere 'twixt earth and sky.

    If only I *felt* less!
I'd be resigned to my dull mind;
    I'd not be such a mess.

    But, as it is, I'm split!
In direst dole's my tortured soul;
    My brains can't rescue it.
        (Gerard Benson)

'How I met . . .' An excerpt from the memoirs of a nobody:

> In my 27 years as barber at the Out and Out Club
> I saw most of the crowned heads of Europe and
> was privileged to wash and cut the hair of many of
> the leading men of the time. Professional
> etiquette prevents me saying much, but I can
> disclose that my most memorable client was the
> then Cardinal Archbishop of Westminster. I will
> always treasure the memory of our first meeting.
> It was an afternoon in late October. As I settled
> him into the chair and did the preliminaries I
> ventured to say, 'The evenings are closing in,
> Your Eminence.' 'Yes, Mr Harbottle,' he replied
> (Harbottle was my predecessor), 'and the clocks
> go back next Sunday.' I often recall what I like to
> think of as the Parable of the Clocks. He was truly
> a Prince amongst churchmen.
>
> (James Comyn)

Items on the agenda of two frightful Festivals:

FILM: *Pavements in Ipswich*—as setting, subject and climax of
still life as drama.

TABLEAU: An exhibition of mid-19th-century Belgian unglazed
pottery.

POETRY: A demonstration of 18th-century hoeing to illustrate the
William McGonagall poem 'On the calamitous disaster befalling
Murdoch McIntosh when he became impaled on his hoe during
a cloudburst in the very bad harvest of 1776'.

MUSIC: Slow dance performed to atonal pipe music whose
funereal ambience symbolises the suffering of the Third World.

(Sheelagh and David Panton)

THE EMPTY ROOM: A new production by the Stavanger Nothing Theatre. No props, no scenery, no actors. Outbecketts Beckett.

BLANK WALLS: Abandoned works by anonymous artists. Stimulating and suggestive.

DESTRUCTS: Dust, shards, ground glass, crushed concrete. Art reduced to its elements.

FROZEN REPOSE: Marathon spectacular by the Staszoanary Dance Group of Outer Siberia.

(Special note: Doors locked during performances. Bars closed at all times.)

(Peter Peterson)

Extracts from the Diary of a Present-day Nobody:

Friday: This morning, found my usual train much shorter than usual; consequently, many persons of obvious second-class status had occupied all the first-class seats. Entering one compartment, I remarked meaningfully: 'This *is* First-Class, you know'—whereupon some uncouth fellow chirped: 'Bright boy—go to the top of the class!' On my further remarking: 'I *trust* everyone here is a First-Class ticket-holder', he riposted: 'Trust on, Sunshine', thereby raising a general guffaw. A saucy young miss giggled: 'Come and sit on my lap, grand-dad' and some other wag grinned: 'Move up for Lord Toffeenose.' But I had had enough and resolved to fetch a ticket inspector. As the corridors were now jam-packed as well, I had to step out onto the platform to do so—whereupon the train promptly shot out of the station, the irregular occupants of *my* compartment giving me an insolent wave and cheer as they flashed past. Really! What *is* England coming to?

(Claude Spettigue)

January 23. Back to work today. Angry scene with NUPE shop steward. He said I should have been on picket duty yesterday. I pointed out that the buses were on strike, I had no petrol because of the tanker drivers' dispute and the trains were not running. He replied that I could have walked. When I said, 'I live ten miles away and in any

(60)

case I'm not a member of NUPE', be became red and strangely speechless. I took advantage of this to tell him that Lupin, although still unemployed, had been very active on several picket lines. For some reason this did not please him. I decided to ignore his remark 'If it wasn't for the ambulance drivers being back today I'd dot you one.' (I have left out some words in case Carrie reads this.) Tonight Lupin asked for £5 for the strike fund. Refused and felt I had dealt a telling blow to NUPE.

(J. Timson)

The most forgettable character I've ever met:

> She's been writing to me every Christmas for
> years. She says she was at school with me and I
> called her Puggy. She says we used to travel
> down from Paddington together and I liked her
> mother's sandwiches. I remember the sandwiches
> —tomato, tomato pickle and onion in brown
> bread—I don't remember Puggy. She says we
> played in *As You Like It* and she was Touchstone
> to my Audrey. I remember playing Audrey, I
> don't remember Touchstone. She says we went
> out on our first date with boys together. I
> remember my first date (I was seduced immediately),
> I don't remember Puggy. I keep meaning to get
> in touch with her, but I always lose her cards
> and forget her address. I wish I remembered Puggy.
>
> (Estelle Holt)

All Things
Are Full of Labour

Students of evening institutes wax poetic about their creations:

That's my first Abstract hanging on the wall,
Looking like a Mondrian; I call
That piece a wonder, now: my eager hands
Worked busily a session—there it stands.
Will't please you sit and look at it? I said
'My eager hands' by design, for never read
Strangers like you that cunning dissonance,
The depth of passion of its utterance,
But to myself they turned (since none puts by
The curtain I have drawn for you but I)
And seemed as they would ask me, if they durst,
How came I by such skill; so, not the first
Are you to turn and ask thus. Sir, 'twas not
My teacher's presence only called that spot
Of colour into lovely being; perhaps
It were immodest to say, 'My genius taps
A spring where Mondrian drank. Nay, let it go
—Yet, I fancy . . . Note the purple, though!
Leave it that genius is a rarity,
And Evening Classes brought it out in me.
                                        (T. Griffiths)

Basket, basket, gaping wide
On the table by my side,
What imperfect industry
Could shape this frightful mystery?

On what crowded pavement gravel
Will your raffia unravel?
Will the shoppers all guffaw
To see this comedy of straw?

When your dye begins to run
What (d)ripping fun for everyone;
And what agony and pain
To have to make you all again.

What the blazes? What's the chances
Of receiving pitying glances?
If I do get funny stares,
I'll give up creels and take to chairs.
(F. J. Tarrant)

Some do-it-yourself poets:

Henry Reed on the Mending of Fuses
Tonight we have mending of fuses. Yesterday
We had cleaning of wastepipes. And tomorrow
   morning
We shall have horrors we dare not imagine. But tonight,
Tonight we have mending of fuses. For
   convenience fuse boxes
Are located in the darkest and most inaccessible
Corners of the domicile. Groping among
   spiders' webs
I know, whichever I choose first, the one wanted
   will be last.

(63)

To effect fuse-mending properly, one needs
    fuse wire.
We ought to have had some somewhere, but
    would have saved an hour
If we had borrowed from next door in the
    first place.
Tonight, after the flash, we shall have mending
    of fuses again
After the mending of plugs, which we could do
If we could remember the wiring, which we
    could do

If we could find the diagram from the
   Electricity Board.
Tomorrow we shall have mending of fuses again
For tonight we shall make do with candles.
                    (Maud Gracechurch)

Gerard Manley Hopkins on Making Scones
My flour fetched, salt-sprinkled, sift in self-
Raised, self-unselving with raisins wrinkle-round:
Soon scones will, kitchen-cosseted, be sudden-found,
The crumble cake-scapes clustered, shaped for shelf.
O fingers linger, tender-tippèd, thus to mix
Thy marge in moist: most need must, mingling, knead.
And ah! in flour sour cream streams! So my creed
Is dough, deft dough, light-hefted, fair to fix.
Now punch-pleased, pat in pattern, pitter-pat,
Cut careful, all board-ordered. Best to bake
Brushed beaten-egg-neat, meet to eat. Lay flat,
Fresh-fashioned passion, gas-mark-eight to take
Ten tongue-tight, frightful minutes, while set platt-
ers placed: such grace my scone-skilled God will make.
                    (Ellen Brigwell)

Praise, Blame,
Love, Kisses, Tears
and Smiles

A new version of Kipling's 'If' addressed exclusively to women:

If you can keep your bra when all about you
   Are burning theirs (and looking dreadful sights),
And yet convince the sisterhood who doubt you
   Of your intense belief in women's rights;
If you can show the men who criticise you
   That body needs the partnership of mind
So subtly as to make them realise you
   Have one of each, and of the finest kind;
If you can tease, and not be sharp or stinging;
   If you can grace, but not depend on, dress;
If you can talk, and make it seem like singing;
   If you can listen without weariness;
If you can please forget for just a minute
   Your Double First, and your Debating Cup,
Yours is my sink and everything that's in it:
   And what is more, I'll do the drying up.
                (Paul Griffin)

Differences between men and women:

Men want to be loved for what they do; women want to be loved
  whatever they do.

Men love women for what they do; women love men whatever
  they do.

Men aren't sexy if they think they are; women aren't sexy unless
  they think they are.

Men love before; women love after.

Men enjoy the hunt; women enjoy the hunt ball.
                (Carole Angier)

Though male and female noses are roughly the same size, there is a vast difference between the handkerchief sizes of the two sexes.
(Joseph Cole)

A woman's ache is a man's incipient coronary thrombosis.
(Alex Campbell)

A woman keeps silent when she is in the right, a man when he is in the wrong.
(John Sweetman)

A man who strays is a bit of a dog; a woman who strays is a complete bitch.
(Sydney Norgate)

Men and women see the funny side of each other, but women conceal their amusement better.
(Julian)

Woman proposes, disposes, imposes, opposes, purposes, supposes, apposes, deposes and exposes; man dozes.
(Ewan Smith)

Men play the game; women know the score.
(Roger Woddis)

Sonnets to poetically neglected bodily features:

On her Nose
Much have I revelled in the realms of flesh,
And many a goodly leg and bottom seen;
Round many twin-peaked headlands have I been
Voyaging, in imagination fresh;
Yet these familiar causes of love's woes
Had wrought satiety and discontent;
I long was stranger to what rapture meant,

(68)

Chloë, until I gazed upon—thy nose.
Then felt I like some watcher of the birds
When a great osprey perches near his hide;
Or like some student architect who girds
His loins to study tricks our fathers tried,
And contemplates, in wonder reft of words,
Some gargoyle arching from a minster's side.
                    (Peter Sheldon)

To an Eyelash

Your well proportioned figure and your face,
Your auburn hair so casually curled,
Are all attractions that would not disgrace
A Grecian goddess or a new Miss World.
I'd sing the praises, if I had the wit,
Of your anatomy—its every part—
But oh! your starboard eyelash is the bit
That more than others captivates my heart.
Its silky lushness, its enchanting curl,
The way it flutters by your damask cheek,
Leave my emotions in a hopeless whirl
And make my knees feel positively weak.
    Just let my lips brush that which I adore—
    Oh! Sorry, girl, I've knocked it on the floor.
                    (George van Schaick)

To his Mistress's Toenail

Like the first flush of morning glimpsed through glass,
Like the veiled petal of the dew-washed rose,
Like the Provençal pool that pinkly flows
Over flamingo feathers as they pass;
Like frosted apple-blossom on the grass,
Or tiny shells that ebbing tides disclose—
Such are the crystal crownings of your toes,
Yet they those common beauties far outclass.
Oh, as I lie a captive at your feet,
Helplessly fettered there by tenfold art,

(69)

Tread not my suffering spirit in the dust!
But if I perish—as at last I must—
Grant me a consummation sharply sweet,
And with one dainty nail impale my heart.
(Mary Holtby)

A Leap Year marriage proposal from a real or imaginary woman in telegram form consisting of 24 words in alphabetical order:

Am being chaste despite entreaties for
grandmother has insisted just keep lovers
meetings nonchalant or pure resisting sinful
temptations until vowing wed your zoe.
(Donald Rayfield)

From Xanthippe to Socrates in Latin (with Mr Howarth's own translation):

Anno Bissextili: care: domo egregia fui graeca: iuvenem, jocosam,
   kariten, laetam, mitem nympham, o philosophe qui recto studes,
   tuam uxorem vis?—Xanthippe zelosa.
(Leap Year: Darling: I come from excellent Greek stock: O
   philosopher zealous for what is right, do you wish for your wife
   a young, gay, gracious, blithe, gentle nymph?—Xanthippe
   burning with passion.)
(J. B. Howarth)

A poet's mistress, reversing the traditional roles, urges him not to propose:

I'll play White Goddess to your Robert Graves,
And place you highest on my list of slaves.
Make me the subject of a villanelle,
A rondeau and a triolet as well,

An epigram, a ballad or a sonnet—
Make me a pedestal and I'll stand on it.
But girls who darn your Y-fronts can't inspire
Your latest ode, or move your muse's lyre.
I've burnt my bra, but I'll not burn my boats.
I want no husband, I've not sown my oats,
I'll choose an undomesticated life;
It's easier being a goddess than a wife.
No, Poet, I'll not share your humble garret,
I'm your Dark Lady, not Elizabeth Barrett.
          (Fiona Pitt-Kethley)

Competitors were asked to add three more verses to Kipling's:
          Roses red and roses white
          Plucked I for my love's delight.
          She would none of all my posies—
          Bade me gather her blue roses . . .

          'Roses blue, my love?' 'Yes, blue.'
          'I'll go search for some.' 'Please do.'
          'If I meet with no success,
          Will you punish me?' 'Oh, yes.'

          All a-tingle I set forth
          To the east, west, south and north.
          Empty-handed home I went
          For the promised punishment.

          It was pleasure intertwined
          With pain (so cruel yet so kind).
          Soon I'm off up to the hills,
          Searching for blue daffodils.
                    (Stanley Shaw)

In a horticultural fog,
I had to get a catalogue;
There I found a rose, *Blue Moon*,
Bought a bush to flower in June.

In the pause before it flowered
Relations with my love quite soured;
I think she thought I wasn't trying,
Told me other chaps were vying.

I heard her ask one wretched fellow
To gather her delphiniums yellow.
Love died away, the rose bloomed grey.
Unnatural practices never pay.
                    (Frances Rhodes)

Poetic advice to a young person about to get married:

The day that I married your mother
    Was the happiest day of her life.
All her subsequent years, she would tell me
    with tears
She knew nothing but sorrow and strife.

Though a fine and intelligent woman,
    She'd a critical nature, you see.
What she criticised most were my temper, my
    toast,
My income, my morals, and me.

Many Thinkers think Marriage immoral;
    Few find it Ineffable Bliss.
If I *had* to advise—which I doubt would be
    wise—
    The advice that I'd give would be this:

Don't marry a man who's a Gargoyle,
  A Gangster, a Goof, or a Gay;
If marry you must, marry one you can trust
  To die on the following day.
              (P.B.)

From marriage both can have their will,
Take what they want, and pay the bill,
Which happily I'm paying still.

Much giving makes a marriage thrive,
But how to take as well as give
Is part of learning how to live.

Choice is the hardest thing by far,
So take my tip: when at the bar
Before the priest or registrar

Look critically to your right
And check that the resulting sight
With whom you plan to spend the night

Will, after fifteen thousand more,
Not have become a tiny bore.
If so, stamp hard upon the floor,
Cry out 'I won't!' and find the door.
              (Paul Griffin)

Competitors were asked for verses for newly-weds on 'How to be Happy though Married':

If you are never tired when she is willing,
And never treat this duty as a chore;
If you've ensured your feet are never chilling,
And taken steps to see you never snore;

If you can wait and never moan while waiting,
As she completes her lipstick—and her eyes;
If you've not heard her nagging or berating,
Nor answered blunt home truths with half-baked lies;

If you have hymned her as the modern Beeton,
Devouring each burnt offering with a will,
Nor left a single uncooked bean uneaten,
Whilst crossing fingers as you praised her skill;
If you have never quarrelled over money,
And paid her bills and never queried why—
You're right to claim that marriage is all honey,
And, what is more, my lad, that pigs can fly.
(Harrison Everard)

A passage from a novel written for sensitive males suffering from the same frustrations as maltreated women struggling for liberation:

Norman sank into his ample armchair. Locked in by his wife, he stared glumly at the television, rubbing the outsize stomach she'd forced him to cultivate—a beer-bulge he'd built up assiduously, hoping to be the butt of cruel jibes. Yet she'd never complained.

He howled inwardly. The carpet was sharp, lacerating his soles, spiking him through his shoes—leather worn away by his perennial pacing, up and down inside the maternity unit.

Compelled by her endless fidelity to take mistresses, browbeaten by her happy housekeeping into working long hours at the office, forced by the local WI to lug cumbersome loads of jam about . . . his was the helpless degradation of manhood.

She sat quietly, knitting his sweaters. And what had she said when he'd called her subservient? 'Darling, you are lovely.' Deep inside, he felt the elastic of his nerves stretch nearer to breaking-point.
(Ellen Brigwell)

Competitors were asked for a poem describing a memorable weekend, beginning, 'Do you remember an inn, Miranda?' (or any other preferred name):

> Do you remember an inn, Ned,
> Beside the sluggish Ouse,
> The wide grey sky, and the pigeon-pie,
> Two very old canoes
> In a corrugated shed
> Behind bamboos?
>
> Do you remember the kisses,
> The novels left unread,
> The moorhens' cry and the clouds piled high,
> The home-made gingerbread?
> And the abundant blisses
> Of that brass bed?
>   (Ginger Jelineck)

A pantoum in celebration of divorce:

At last I have got my decree,
It's all over, just see if I care,
There are plenty of fish in the sea,
And the world's full of birds free as air.

It's all over, just see if I care,
Everywhere there's fruit ripe for the fall,
And the world's full of birds free as air,
They're just waiting to come to my call.

Everywhere there's fruit ripe for the fall,
My experienced touch will deceive 'em,
They're just waiting to come to my call.
Ah, how coldly I'll love 'em and leave 'em.

My experienced touch will deceive 'em,
There'll be no one to please but myself,
Ah, how coldly I'll love 'em and leave 'em,
Now I'm all on my own on the shelf.

There'll be no one to please but myself,
There are plenty of fish in the sea,
Now I'm all on my own on the shelf,
At last I have got my decree.
                         (Adam Khan)

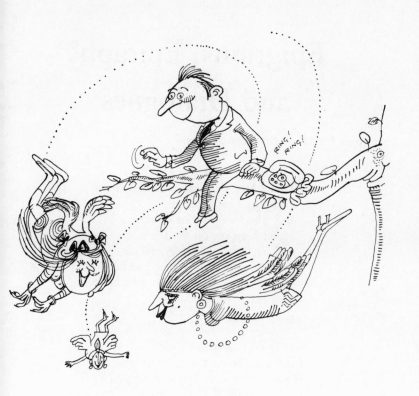

Epigrams, Epitaphs and Dialogues

Mottoes for useful everyday objects:

Mirror

Take heart, dear girl, and find in me
a shining new identity—
and when we start to disagree
    just keep me on the shelf
and dust my ageless face to see
the You you always meant to be:
look when you must, and then be free
    to trust yourself.
        (Gina Berkeley)

Alarm Clock

I did not choose the hour to wake you:
If you rise not, I cannot make you.
        (E. S. Goodwill)

Coffee Percolator

Fit for a stately home that stands
    In its own grounds, I see
No cause to envy house or lands—
    My own grounds stand in me.
        (Tony Brode)

Spectacles

Beware! The world I show can turn your mind;
It has no gentle blur of love or charity.

Look briefly. Much is better undefined.
Only opticians set their hearts on clarity.
(Paul Griffin)

Umbrella
Unfurled I shield the rainswept masses;
Well rolled I mark the ruling classes.
(Kate Short)

Very modern epitaphs:

Samaritan
Here lies a man who often sat
And listened on the phone
To those with lives so awful that
At last he took his own.
(Joyce Johnson)

Marriage Counsellor
For better or for worse he's tied
To death, and sees the other side.
(George Moor)

Disc Jockey
Unfailingly benign and brisk,
No more may he beguile us,
Rolled round on earth's rotating disc
Till Doomsday raise the stylus.
(Moyra Blyth)

Travel Agent
After a lifetime packaging vacations
(To Mykonos, Minorca and Lucerne),
John Smith has now confirmed his reservations
To the bourne from which no traveller may return.
(G. Waldman)

Bank-robber

Beneath this mound, a bank he cannot rob,
He lies; he wore a stocking 'on the job',
But Death has given him a final sock
And softly, softly turned the prison lock.
(P.M.)

Stripper

She shed her clothes with such abandon
That no one knew which lap they'd land on;
Now scattered on this lap of earth
Is all the gear she had from birth—
Her supple flesh, eyes, teeth and curls:
She has outstripped the other girls.
(P.M.)

Porn-peddler

Here lies Nature's pet aversion,
Millionaire through sex perversion.
Now behold this little squirt
Buried in a mound of dirt.
(P. M. Cook)

A dialogue between two people of different historical periods, each using slang of his own generation:

YOBBO: Farkinell! What's this freak then? New Romantic?
GOBBO: Back, coxcomb! I'll be sworne thou'rt more fiend than *Angedeciel* (as the fantastical French do appellate) and more knave than fiend, hung all about with fetters like gibbet meat.
Y: Stone me! You got the verbals alright, in't yer?
G: What manner of cully art thou, parrot poll?
Y: Ain't yer never seed a punk?
G: Punks, drabs and swagbelly whores by the cartload, but none so fashioned. Thou'rt prickt out for *altera res*.
Y: Yeah? Well, mate, I'm a punk, i'n I?

G: A base scallawag ingle. (I'll firk him.) Art thou meet for a
   tumble? A figo for thee!
Y: Get stuffed.
G: An thou'lt supplie the sage and onions.
Y: Piss off, weirdo!
G: Adieu, petit perroquet. Joie of thy punkadilloes!
                                        (Gerard Benson)

Samples of quintessentially marital dialogue:

> 'What shall I wear on Tuesday?'
> 'I'm not a clairvoyant, dear.'
> 'Oh come on!'
> 'Put on the gold then.'
> 'You must be joking!'
> 'Well, wear the blue.'
> 'Listen, Dumb-bell, long skirts went out with the ark.'
> 'I wonder what she'll give us this time?'
> 'Something revolting in oil or cheese.'
> 'Oh God! I don't believe it.'
> 'You could always have flu again.'
> 'No chance; anyway, you're driving this time.
> Remember?'
> 'That cobweb's still on the ceiling.'
> 'Get rid of it then.'
> 'If I had arms that long, I'd be working in a
> circus.'
> 'At least you'd be working.'
> 'Oh! Tremendous. You'll wash up for that.'
> 'After the News, dear.'
> 'I think I'll go topless.'
> 'Why not indeed?'
> 'On second thoughts, I'll wear the gold.'
>   (Alma Hill)

'Hello, darling. Was that you before?'
'Uhu.'
'What happened?'
'The machine ate my money.'
'You got the operator?'
'Uhu.'
'Where are you?'
'At Klong's.'
'Why there?'
'Wanted to see Boffy about the phrontistery.'
'Anything nice?'
'Only if you like schlock . . . anyway, how are you
    today?'
'Fine, fine. You sound gronky.'
'Bit stanco—been on the whizz all day; what have
you been up to?'
'Oh, the usual, lying on my chaise-longue and
eating turkish delight. What're you doing now?'
'Back to't mill.'
'Take it easy. Usual time tonight?'
'Yes: dropping in at the doghouse on the way home.'
'Well, don't eat any sausage custard: take care.'
'You take care too. Bye.'

(Lionel Burman)

*An imaginary dialogue between an English Queen and an intruder
into the royal bedchamber:*

Q: Unbed thee, saucy sirrah!
I: I seek but to converse and set the time free from tediousness.
Q: Why must thy tediousness disturb my time of sleep?
I lay but now in Morpheus' arms.
I: Pardon, lady, I saw him not. I had thought to find
a solitary and virgin Queen.
Q: Thou art a Greekless, witless knave. Dost thou

(82)

assail my solitude and my virginity?
I: The former only, gentle madam. I crave a boon.
'Tis bruited abroad that Ralegh, late from the Indies,
hath brought a fragrant plant whose conflagration
gratifies the nostrils.
Q: Rumour hath wronged thee. The vile potato
pleaseth neither nose nor eye.
I: Nay, 'tis a leaf I crave and not a root.
Q: Ah, now I know thy fumous want! Straight from
the neighbour chamber, where Essex lies exhausted,
I'll fetch thee one.

(D. P. M. Michael)

*Competitors were asked for a conversation in which members of a
family hint at the presents they would like to receive:*

GERALD: Gosh! You smell divine.
VERA: The last of my Chanel No. 5. Cigarette?
GERALD: Thanks. Match? Your hand *is* cold!
VERA: It's bitter out, and I've a hole in my best gloves.
GERALD: Drink? Sorry about the odd glasses.
VERA: Why apologise? You haven't for the odd socks.
GERALD: Sorry. I haven't done the washing for a couple of days.
  Where shall we go?
VERA: Nowhere so classy that my old coat will be shown up
  among a lot of mink and silver foxes.
GERALD: I wouldn't have suggested it. I'm reduced to my last
  clean shirt. And with odd cuff-links. How much time have we?
VERA: I'm not sure. Mummy's claimed her watch back.
GERALD: I'll check on the radio—if the old thing's working.
  What about going to that new film at the ABC? They say the
  book was fabulous.
VERA: I know. I heard the record of the music round at Janet's.

(Maud Gracechurch)

A conversation between Man and God:

Our Christmas guests got tight on gin.
'Oh God,' I said and God said, 'Yes?'
Which rather put me in a spin
For I was tongue-tied more or less.

I blurted out, 'The weather's warm
With Christmas Eve already here.'
He said, 'Yes, hardly true to form.'
I said, 'We'll pay for it, I fear.'

'Ah well,' he sighed, 'I must get on,
But thanks for sparing time to chat.'
I should have mentioned Christ His Son.
But He had gone and that was that.
                    (Gerry Hamill)

And Here
the Poet Meets His
Favouring Muse

As contemporary poets are often criticised for the triviality of their subject matter, a sonnet on the universe was demanded:

What galaxies delighted Adam's sight?
Did Pegasus blaze square across night's blue?
Was Venus visible to Eve's rapt view,
In transcendental incandescent light?
What colours burned those stellar fires mint-bright?
Did pure Arcturus gleam pale gold when new?
Betelgeuse glow wine-red? We have no clue
To these and future mysteries of the night.

Great satellites, multiplied thousand-fold,
Piercing dark astronomic miles of space,
In years to come may fascinate men's eyes,
Braiding the stars with gold; and they may trace
Fresh hieroglyphs of fire in those skies
So differently damascened of old.

(Adrienne Gascoigne)

An unseasonable poem in dispraise of Christmas:

Alas, the time is come again
To make the sacred more profane,
To summon up the festive zeal,
The bonhomie one does not feel,

Time to fix the idiot grin
As ghastly Christmas gifts roll in,
And from their gaudy wrappings creep
Evil things that burp and bleep.
Once more on TV screens appear
Worn-out films of yesteryear,
Cards arrive from persons who
Will not be blessed with one from you,
Feuds, preserved with loving care,
Wither in the hate-starved air.
The saints preserve us through this season
That plunders pockets, peace, and reason!
(Philip A. Nicholson)

Two parodies of a typical Georgian poem:

Over the sleeping winter trees
Rises smoke from cottage hearth
Blue and straight; there is no breeze.
Hoar-frost powders the spinney path.

Gracefully, she steps along;
From afar I see her eyes.
My heart leaps with quiet song;
Along the shore a curlew cries.

The withered stump that guards the lawn
Welcomes my Love with ivied arm:
She spurns my hand this winter morn
And passes by with haughty charm.

They say that once the heart is lost
Love makes a slave of the hardest-bitten;
I count it gain and little cost,
To be the bondman of a kitten.
(T. Griffiths)

Such was the bounty of that Sussex June:
Bold-painted butterflies, the mellow tune
Of ball on seasoned willow, raucous caws
Of sober-suited rooks the sole applause
Our prowess earned or craved. Elysian day!
And as we sped its golden hours away,
United in the brotherhood of cricket,
Our burly blacksmith bowled and Squire kept wicket;
And only when the light began to fail
Could stumps at last be drawn. Then goodly ale
Filled tankard after foaming tankard, laughter's
Friendly din assailed the tavern's rafters
And each man thrilled with uttermost content;
A span of quintessential summer, spent
In comradeship amid the gentle arts
Of English landscape, blessed by English hearts.
(Martin Fagg)

Some 'streaking' poems:

Streak, streak, streak,
O'er the cool gray stones, whoopee!
And count not the eyes that are staring
At bold little, cold little me.

O well for the constable lad,
All stiff and official and glum!
O well for the constable's dog,
With undisciplined craving for bum!

Streak, streak, streak,
For we're prophets of freedom, not freaks,
And only the fangs of a frenzied hound,
Can e'er bring a blush to *my* cheeks.
(R. J. Steel)

Wee, sleekit, far frae tim'rous streaker,
I ken ye dinna mind a keeker,
But och! Can onything be bleaker
   Than that blue skin!
I doot ye need a brimmin' beaker
   Tae help ye rin.

Puir thing! I wunner why ye dae it.
The fashion? What a price tae pay it!
Ye think ye're braw? No, lass, far frae it—
   It's juist vexation
That even for me, lass—daur I say it?
   Ye're nae temptation.
          (Dromore)

Had I but Lust enough and Leisure
This streaking, lady, were a Pleasure.
We should shed clothes and think which way
T'amaze the vulgar with our play.
Thou by the Serpentine's slow tide
Shouldst Coppers tempt, I by thy side . . .
But at my back I seem to hear
The Black Marias hurrying near,
And yonder all before us waits
The hungry Maw of Magistrates.
Then the dim bench shall rudely try
That dazzling flaming nudity,
Humbling thy beauties to the dust
And making vanish all my Lust.
Wandsworth's a fine and private place
But only men do there embrace.
          (Celia Haddon)

A Gilbertian song for a modern judge:

Though a Judge's robe is splendid, if a man aspires to fill it, he
Must cultivate an air of polymathic versatility.
I am trendy, I am swinging: outside Caxton Hall the traffic'll
Be thick when I am lecturing on problems pornographical.
I have been to *Oh! Calcutta!* I've a pretty taste in nudities,
I blush at no four-letter word, however coarse and crude it is.
On the ethics of abortion I know more than you'd expect o' me;
I'm a recognised authority on painless hysterectomy.
On a television panel I can puzzle and perplex you all
With my avant-garde opinions upon matters homosexual;
I can chat with Brigid Brophy about mysteries obstetrical,
And remember more of Ireland's woes than Lynch or Bernadette
    recall,
Though Society's permissive, I can see no grounds to curb it on;
I can quote you the statistics on wife-swapping down in
    Surbiton.
On the Bench I'm really with it—no judicial whims or
    waggeries:
I do *not* say 'What's a rave-up?' and I *never* ask who Jagger is.
After half a day's Inquiry, I can tell you what the answer is
To questions that have baffled all the European Chanceries.
I take evidence from students at a demo or a palisade,
And I hear about the sit-ins that they plan with Tariq Ali's aid.
When a strike occurs, or arguments on salaries or debts arise,
I pronounce my magic formula, and everybody gets a rise.
Oh, from Town and Country Planning to the Min. of Ag. and
    Fishery
I'm the paragon and pattern of Her Majesty's Judiciary!
                    (Robin A. Henderson)

Competitors were asked for a poem with 16 given rhymes (taken from Don Juan, *Canto* XVI, *Stanzas 32–3):*

'My hands shake when I try to hold them still,
And as for sleeping, well, I've more or less
Resigned myself, you know . . . I feel quite ill,
Mainly on Fridays when it comes out . . . Yes,
That's right, the competition tests one's skill
At wrenching words about till they express
With wit or wisdom what's been asked for . . . Tell
Me straight, Doc. When will I be really well?'

'Such cases are, I fear, mysterious;
The competition addict can be both
Extremely lucid and delirious.
The obsession shows a characteristic growth:
At first a bit of fun, it gets more serious
Until at last the gibbering victim's loath
To eat or sleep . . . I say, I took for granted
The plain, unvarnished truth was what you wanted?'
                              (Peter Norman)

And I shall remember you still,
Although you may love me the less:
Would I do you a positive ill?
The answer's a negative 'yes'.
The doctor who loses his skill,
The poet who cannot express
The thoughts he is burning to tell,
Are losers and winners as well.

The bonds of the heart are mysterious,
They comfort and strangulate both;
When happiness seems most delirious,
It signals the end of its growth.

The clown bringing laughter is serious,
The passionate lover is loath
To take easy favours when granted,
And what is most sought is least wanted.
(Roger Woddis)

On 'Beachcomber'

Say not that voice is mute, for ever still;
The age it mirrored needed it far less
Than we who now are suffering ill on ill.
We need its honesty and humour—yes,
Almost alone it had an arcane skill;
In simple, jesting words it could express
Contempt or love—above all, it could tell
Its sorrows for the land it served so well.

Perhaps the art was not mysterious;
Its heirs could carry on the craft—be both
Precise and brief, excise delirious
And esoteric verbiage, whose growth
Has made the outlook for our tongue so serious.
Send back that chuckling voice. It would be loath
To take our present sorry State for granted;
It should be combing beaches where it's wanted.
(I. C. Snell)

Competitors were asked to expand a single-line poem by Gavin Ewart: 'A tie, in dining cars, commands respect.'

'A tie, in dining cars, commands respect,'
My father tells me, straightening my own.
'The waiters everywhere in France expect
A schoolboy to possess an adult's tone . . .
Sarah's ready now. Wash, and brush your hair.'
Sliding the door, she smiles: he takes her arm—
We sit, he talks, and picks a wine that's rare.

The waiter bows: *'Et pour après, madame?'*
Between each course she smokes, and drops her ash
Among the broken bread and in the wine.
She watches me, and I glance back, abashed.
'Darling,' he kisses her, 'smile—Sarah mine.'
Stealthily, for me, he strokes her thigh,
Silently loosening the marriage-tie.
(Anna Gramm)

A tie, in dining cars, commands respect,
But not unless its use is quite correct.
Last Wednesday, on the train to Aberdeen,
At lunch, I witnessed a revolting scene:
A fat man sitting opposite was dressed
In flannel trousers and an old string vest,
Yet still he wore *a tie* of bright green wool,
And then, while waiting for his plate to cool,
Removed it, tied it in a simple loop,
And nonchalantly dipped it in his soup,
Then took it out and sucked his soup from it.
But I did not enjoy my soup a bit.
(Michael Pickering)

Some 'double haikus' with themes of equal interest to both East and West:

I want a posh death;
Choir singing their balls off,
Me, sharp as a sheath,
Starch-stiff in my box,
White tie, tails and rhinestone pin;
Heaps of grief-mad kin.
(Russell Lucas)

'Homosexual'
Sounds somehow so clinical,

(92)

While 'gay' is absurd.
'Queer' seems daft for chaps
So frequently found. Perhaps
There *is* no right word.
   (Andrew McEvoy)

Sun and Wind and Rain,
Hunger, Cold and Poverty,
Sorrow, Death and Pain,
Ours or another's,
Good Saint Francis called them all
Sisters and Brothers.
   (Joyce Johnson)

The fickle wind heaped
Pale petalled drifts on the grass
Torn from the peach tree.
When autumn was ripe
My lover went on his way
Thirsty for peaches.
  (Maureen McBain)

Without my glasses
I fancy all the lasses
Are smiling at me.
I'm eager to see,
So I put my glasses on . . .
The smiles are all gone.
  (Barney Blackley)

In praise of the lavatory:

Thine, Lord, the Chain of Circumstance,
Beneath Thy Seat the Waters fall,
Creation's first flush Thine, for Thee
Rises and sinks the Earthly Ball.

He, Lord, who followed Thy Design
Has now no mere Terrestrial Throne,
But in Thy Many-Mansioned House
One Private Room is all his own.
                              (John N. Wales)

We didn't mention our bodies
When I was a shy little lad,
So, often, avoiding the ladies
I went to the Place by the shed.

You had to step over the mower
And sit in an odour of coir;
There were gardening gloves, a dried flower,
And a draught coming under the door.

A patch of the whitewash was peeling;
There were cobwebs over the wall;
The cistern protested at pulling
And clunked when the thingummy fell.

But the song of the birds in the garden
Made dreams come alive in my head
As I felt the relief from my burden,
The escape from the mess we have made.
                              (Paul Griffin)

Two fables in which the protagonist follows the advice of a proverb and comes to a sticky end:

'See a pin and pick it up,' they say,
'And through the day you're visited by luck.'
The bent nail sends the tenor on his way,
Steering him safe through Verdi, Wagner,
　Gluck.

A pin, or nail, or some approximation,
Is sure to help the one by whom it's found;
And more, the system is not bound by nation:
A pin is a pin is a pin the whole world round.

With this in mind Our Hero smiled a smile.
A pin! For a whole day his luck was made!
He soon lay spread across a good square mile,
For he had failed to spot the hand grenade.
　　　　　　(John McPherson)

'Everything comes to him who waits',
Young Ralph was made to understand.
He could rely on kindly Fate's
Bestowal of a winning hand.

At twenty-one it seemed too soon:
To rise and act was premature.
If not the morning, afternoon
Would bring the postman's knock for sure.

At forty-five the Jungle Beast
Was silent, hidden in its lair.
Was Ralph perturbed? Not in the least.
His Karma lay ahead, somewhere.

They buried Ralph at eighty-three.
Obituaries, though brief, were fond;
For no one doubts that Destiny
Awaits him in the Great Beyond.
                    (Basil Ransome-Davies)

Sunday morning:

These I have loved: the gradual waking;
That serene,
Slack sense of hours that, shaking
Off the harness of routine,
Follow their own free path;
The long luxuriant bath
Listening to *The Archers*—whose quintessential triteness
Brings brightness
To the most weary sophisticate;
Then breakfast—a modest one, for weight
Must be regarded—so simply egg and bacon, fried bread,
    tomatoes,
Mushrooms, kidneys and fried potatoes,
Endless coffee and cream, and, at the most,
Twelve slices of toast,
Butter and Oxford marmalade, and then a wash
Of colour supplements, garish tosh
That pushes wares
I do not wish to own. Eleven—time for coffee and eclairs,
While on Radio Three the critics shrilly chatter
Of Buxtehude's Fugues and Schumann's *Albumblätter* . . .
                    (Martin Fagg)

This slim cantle of time, which church bells slice
Out of the swollen week, I wish to savour
At pensioner's pace. My Sunday thoughts entice
The hallowed suburb to yield up its flavour.

Sweet Larkin, Betjeman and Christ
Bless this garden, grant me idleness.
For these lax hours, how much I've sacrificed,
Prophet imprisoned in commuter's dress . . .

Gossiping leaves incite the grass to grow;
The mower almost edges to my hand,
Neighbours by their gleaming cars all show
How bright the haloes in this pagan land.

The proud three-litre must be washed of sin,
The flush repaired. On top of other ills
Guests congregate, partaking of my gin:
Bells mock our leisure in the Surrey hills.
(H. B. Mallalieu)

Replies to poetry's unanswered questions:

Do you remember an inn, Miranda?

Not the inn, nor the place,
Nor the dance, nor your face,
Nor the fleas. Will you please
Understand that I'm ageing, bourgeois, and am waging
A war to keep up
(On income diminished, I'm socially finished and lonely as hell);
That the girl who went prancing and glancing and dancing
Through your fields of wild oats
Was not I.
I'm lined and refined and my husband is kind
But quite cold.
A wife who has bedded on straw in the raw he'd abhor.
'Tis a lie, 'twasn't I;
Ask no more.
(Mrs M. G. Lloyd)

Oh what can ail thee, knight at arms
  Alone and palely loitering?
—I suffer intestinal qualms
  And heartburn's sting.

These haggard cheeks, this fevered brow
  My inner turbulence proclaim,
And antiperistalsis now
  'S my only aim.

Last night my military mates
  And I made merry in the Mess;
Ah, he who so participates
  Should shun excess!

The blushful Hippocrene flowed on,
  I leapt the chairs a shade too quick—
And that is why I look so wan
  And feel so sick.
                    (Mary Holtby)

Omnium-Gatherum

Some useless proverbs:

Even the dumbest blonde can shake her head.
(Richard Probyn)

It's a straight road that has no turning.
(Ian Kelso)

Even an ex-wife has a sex life.
(John M. Bennett)

Even the weather forecaster gets wet in the rain.
(John E. Brown)

It takes a big man to blow through the wrong end of a tuba.
(Professor Dana S. Scott)

One glass eye is better than double vision.
(Canon P. A. Schofield)

Show me a man's footprint and I will tell you the shape of his foot.
(F. J. A. Cruso)

If God had meant us to walk, He would have given us shoes.
(Arthur J. Morgan)

A poem describing the characteristics of those born under the 12 zodiacal signs:

An astrological array
Of children meet one rainy day.
What can they do? In each lies hope,
But each is limited in scope.

Leo wants to run the show,
Despite assertive Scorpio;
Sagittarius cannot stand
The limitations they have planned,
And Cancer's blind, protective heart
Takes little Libra's timid part,
While bold Aquarius, keen to shine,
Favours an independent line.
Gemini, keen all parts to take,
Gives worried Virgo stomach-ache;
Creative Pisces, odd and curt,
Broods upon some imagined hurt;
And Aries, standing on his head,
Falls down and has to go to bed.
As lonely as when he was born,
Off goes ambitious Capricorn,
And in a quiet corner meets
Greedy Taurus sucking sweets.
When these grow up, the world, I guess,
Will still be in a frightful mess.

(Paul Griffin)

Instructions in 'gobbledygook' which make the performance of simple tasks near-impossible:

1. Grip the outer sleeve firmly in the left hand with the box's longer axis running diagonally.
2. With the right thumb slide out the inner reticule. STOP IMMEDIATELY if the box is upside down.
3. Use the right thumb and forefinger to extract one SUPA VESTA and hold with the blue combustible knob outermost.
4. Return the reticule with the left-hand index finger. Twist the box through 90° to expose one of the special abrasive strips.
5. Place the blue combustible knob on the near end of the abrasive strip. Slide the knob along the strip.

For the necessary acceleration, begin with the right wrist cocked inwards and let it unwind briskly but naturally. (DO NOT FORCE at this point.) When the knob has covered not less than half *and not more than four-sevenths* of the strip, flick it forward, simultaneously imparting a contrary motion to the box by a free-flowing torque of the left elbow.

Your SUPA VESTA should now be alight.

(G. H. Harris)

Place Foot M (found at base of leg T) into shoe P. (WARNING: Confusing M and N may result in acute pain and ultimately deformity.) Grasp ends A and B of lace R. Pass end A over end B, then loop under. Pull A and B tightly. Take end B (in former position of end A) and, wrapping round right thumb H, form loop pinched between left-hand fingers C and D (illustrated). Take end A (in former position of end B), loop over and under loop held by C and D. Pull both loops gently. If result does not satisfy, do *not* tug ends A or B. Merely take scissors X (not included) and cut vigorously at point Z.

(Simon Rose)

In future, doctors from overseas are to be given tests in English which will include colloquialisms. An extract from the exam:

Question: What treatment would you propose for a patient who thought he was Mutt and Jeff, and frequently felt Tom and Dick?

Answer: Back in Aussie, we don't molly about with these split-personality nuts, or schizophrenics as we call them if we can spell it. Straight off to the shrink. Unless, of course, they're Pommy pollys with good lawyers.

As for Thomas and Richard, bonzer for them if that's what turns them on and they're consenting adults. All the more sheilas for us straight blokes.

(I. C. Snell)

Three 'short short stories', like Maugham's 'The Hairless Mexican'
beginning with the question: 'Do you like macaroni?' and ending with
the exclamation: 'You bloody fool, you killed the wrong man!'

'Do you like macaroni?' asked Emperor Bokassa with an ingratiating smile. I knew it was a trick question. My short term of service as equerry to this great fellow Napoleon-enthusiast had taught me the danger of favouring any cuisine but that of France.

But, with charming illogic, the Emperor made one exception to his own rule—tonight's sumptuous Austerlitz banquet was to be a meal with a difference. A trumpet sounded and a bevy of servants struggled in bearing, as we had been warned it would, a fully cooked colonel of the Palace Guard, recently disgraced, face downwards upon the vegetables. ('An army marches on its stomach,' joked the Emperor indulgently.)

The bearers approached the dais, preceded by a beaming chef. As they drew nearer, however, the smile on the Emperor's face suddenly froze. Yes . . . the body was distinctly *white*, the bald pate, the high forehead and the aristocratic features were disquietingly familiar—they had slaughtered our guest of honour, the President of the French Republic, 'the Empire's greatest friend in Europe'.

Looking blacker than ever, the Emperor leapt forward and seized the miserable chef by his hair: 'You bloody fool, you killed the wrong man!'

(C. H. Moore)

'Do you like macaroni?' said Mrs Armitage.

The oriental gentleman smiled politely, but his eyes were expressionless.

'Yes, indeed, all pasta excellent.'

'The Mozzarella cheese makes all the difference,' said Hugh Grist, the fourth member of the party.

John Armitage poured the Orvieto secco and raised his glass. 'Success to our enterprise.'

'Orvieto cathedral very beautiful,' observed Mr Hu.

The conversation was desultory, each member preoccupied with private speculation.

The Armitages were waiting for the code phrase, but both their guests seemed relaxed and neither showed his hand. As coffee was served, Hugh and Mary exchanged glances—still no sign.

'Cognac?' said John.

'Not for me, thank you—doctor's orders', responded Mr Grist and Mr Hu, in unison.

Dead silence—then all laughed.

'Some more coffee then?' said Mary.

'Thank you, please', said Mr Hu. 'No more thanks' from Grist. Mary refilled Mr Hu's cup, and he drank in silence, smiled and said, 'And now if you excuse, please.' He rose, bowed and collapsed.

Grist covered the Armitages with his Luger.

'One move and you're dead!'

John turned to Mary.

'You bloody fool, you killed the wrong man!'

(Philip Peacock)

'Do you like macaroni?'

'Mickey Rooney? A fine talent ruined by Hollywood.'

It was the sort of reply I had expected. When X was 'Herman', an unsuccessful comedian, it was my task to feed him wisecracks.

X was the most baffling case I had dealt with during my career as a psychiatrist. Forty-seven separate personalities, including an elderly couple whose marriage was failing, now inhabited his unremarkable frame.

Suddenly X's own voice addressed me:

'I had forty-eight personalities. Where's Eddie?'

'Eddie' had been a ruthless tycoon.

'We agreed—' I began.

'You killed him with your damned hypnosis!'

'It was for your own good,' I said. 'Eddie was becoming too dominant.'

'But he had plans for me. I was going to be big, he said, really big. First a book, with a promotional tour. Then the Parkinson Show. After that there'd be a film. Finney might be interested, he said. Just think! I'd show Sybil where she got off!'

X started to weep.

'Why didn't you kill Herman?' he sobbed. 'His stupid jokes are driving me mad!'

Then, with explosive energy, he lunged across the desk at me and screamed, 'You bloody fool, you killed the wrong man!'

(Peter McGivern)

Two newspaper headlines, 'Mayoress strips off at Tory social night' and 'Vague vicar quits after complaints', are supplied with fuller reports:

Petite brunette Mrs Juniper has lashed back at critics claiming she has offended Hellstone ratepayers.

'It's what Conservatism is about,' she told me. 'Caring. I could never stand by and watch a duck or whale drown. Some people don't realise, but they can drown just like us.'

Seeing a baby whale in difficulties, Mrs Juniper, despite being about to respond to the loyal toast, dove into the raging winter sea, hauled a young whale to a rock and administered the kiss of life.

'I was too intent to notice the cold. The whale was quite small. Besides, my husband plays rugger,' said Mrs Juniper. 'I am a regular church-goer and committed Christian. I would do it again.'

(George Moor)

In a sensational development of the row surrounding the rector of St Swithin's, Lower Plumpton, local folk were last night informed that their priest had handed in his notice. The Reverend Arthur Collins has come in for sharp criticism in recent weeks, after he told a stunned congregation he was 'vaguely interested in the Bible'. Interviewed on local radio, he explained: 'I am not too sure how to put this, but the Bible may have something to do with God, and it is probably a book I should read more of.' Asked how much he had read, he announced that he had become rather bogged down in Leviticus. 'It is pretty vague stuff, I think,' he added. But he could 'see some relevance in the earlier books'.

(Belle R. Welling)

The Secretary of the Victoria Association for Greater Understanding and Empathy blasted critics at a press conference today.

'VAGUE's aims have been wilfully misinterpreted,' said the Revd Ron Gonad. 'We have been solely concerned with spiritual welfare, and it is quite untrue that we were running a call-girl network for profit.'

He went on to say that he had been unable to reply to accusations before because a series of minor illnesses had confined him to bed. 'But now I'm fighting fit,' added Ron, 'and those who have spread a lot of dingo's kidneys about me had better watch out.'

It was later learned that the houses of several of VAGUE's leading opponents had been burned down, with heavy loss of life. Asked to comment, Ron would only say, 'I consider that makes us quits.'

State police are investigating.

(Basil Ransome-Davies)

A damning theatrical review so written that a cunning selection could produce the impression of a rave notice for the billboards outside the theatre:

This revival must take pride of place in any catalogue of theatrical disasters. *I cannot recall a production where* turgid *writing*, unconvincing *acting* and ham-fisted *direction combined in so complete* and ludicrous *a whole. The plot is truly amazing* in its ineptitude *and must be without equal in theatre history* for banality.

As a masterful hero, Jeremy Peskett gives a remarkable portrayal of bumbling incompetence and I can just believe that *Pearl Button was ideally cast* as the fresh young ballerina when she first played the part thirty years ago.

Altogether a moving experience, judging by the number of first-nighters who moved out into the bars. If you feel *you must see this* debacle, I should *hurry*—it won't survive the week.

(George van Schaick)

Some more Commandments, such as might have been handed to Sir Edmund Hillary on the top of Everest and subsequently dropped and lost:

You'll interact with females and kids on a fully one-to-one togetherist basis.

You'll relate to your relevant god/allah/buddha/shami/world-process figure with ecumenical supportivefulness.

You'll communicate with your g/a/b/etc figure as an interpersonal friend without old-fashioned hierarchical semiotic structures.

You'll not fail to observe the 35-hour-a-week labour-paradigm.

You'll hold a dialogue with all parent-units integratively.

You'll not get into causing passing-away contexts.

You'll not two-time your current partner unless socially viable.

You'll avoid anti-societal-property-deprivation-related interfaces.

You'll not scandal-monger about your comrades.

You'll not gazump people in a next-door situation or entice their pets away.

(Ron Jowker)

Thou shalt be laid back.

Thou shalt avoid stressful interpersonal relationships.

Thou shalt not be manipulative of others.

Thou shalt hang not only loose but in there.

Thou shalt contrive to thine own self to be good, never mind true.

(Susan H. Llewellyn)

Keep this lot where you can see it, not like the last.
(George Moor)

Two imaginary extracts from Hansard *which capture the rich and rare flavour of our Upper House at full moon:*

Opening the debate on the Marine Wildlife Protection Bill, *Lord*

Bramble (C) said that octopi, despite their poor public image, would be included among the protected species. *Lord Snape* (SDP) objected that, the word octopus being derived from Greek, not Latin, the plural should properly be octopoi, or perhaps octopodes. *Lord Snell of Wigan* (Lab) said that, not having had the benefit of a classical education, he was in no position to arbitrate between the Noble Lords, but personally he was no upholder of foreign plurals and would prefer octopusses, though whether with two s's or three he was uncertain. *Lord Bramble* (C) replied that three s's would be letting the cat out of the bag with a vengeance. (Laughter.) *Lady Melkstone of Borthwick* (SDP) suggested that the Bill be given a second reading, with a dictionary.

(Peter Peterson)

Lord Amboys objected that, be that as it might, the gillie could not enter the Chamber to put his leg in the man-trap as he was not a Peer of the Realm. He would not, he added, have any objection to a live bear, horse or dog being admitted for such a purpose. (Cries of 'Shame!')

The Duke of Atholl argued that a horse would have to be shot, whereas for a Highlander a broken leg was an everyday triviality. *The Bishop of Rochester* said that he had lost a leg to a crocodile while engaged in evangelical work in his youth and volunteered, in the interests of religion and the defence of property, to insert the insensible wooden replacement in the man-trap.

(George Moor)

Intelligible and entertaining prose, the first word beginning with a, the second with b and so on through the alphabet, twice or thrice:

A big cannabis deal—extra fine ganja—has its joys, kid. Like my new opium pipe? Queer, really. Sometimes time undergoes very weird expansions—yawns, zooms, amplifies. But conversely, days elapse fast. Great. Heroin is junk. Killing. Literally. Moderate nips of pot quite rapidly soothe tension, unlike violent wild excesses. Your zip's agape, banana chops. Does Euclid furnish geometric harmony?

Imponderable. Jesus knows. Let's move. No. Oh, peace, quiet, rest, sleep. Terminal unconsciousness. Valhalla will expect you. Zzzz. . .

(Basil Ransome-Davies)

As 'Boz' Charles Dickens exposed facts, giving his initial journalism knowledgeability. Lesser Mayhews, newspapermen of poorer quality, regularly shirked the underworld vileness which existed; yet zealously, as brave crusaders do (even for gain), he investigated jostling, kaleidoscopic London. Maybe no one person, *qua* reporter, so triumphantly upset Victorian world-views, except—yes—Zola.

(Jim Ledbury)

A Bactrian camel doesn't easily find grass. However, inside Jammu, Kashmir, low mountains neighbour open plains. Quite rich slopes tumble under villages where extraordinary yews zoom above bivouacking caravans. Dromedaries eagerly fill grateful humps. Idly jesting, kindly leaders mash nuts or, pondering, quietly roast supper. Their ungulates vastly will excel your zoo animals.

By candlelight, drivers evidently find great happiness in judiciously kidding liberally mixed nationalities. Often Powindahs, quaint rustics speaking tongues unknown, vie with excellent young Zoroastrians.

(Paul Griffin)

A blue-stocking conversation developed. Eileen found GBS humdrum, indigestibly jejune; Karen loathed musicals (notably *Oliver*); Phyllis quite ruthlessly savaged Tourneur ('unbearably vulgar wit . . . extravagant yowling . . . zero actability'); Bertha complimented Dryden's 'emergent feminism'. Gertrude (hopefully in jest) knocked *Lear* mercilessly; Norma overreacted, praising (*qua* respondent) Shakespeare's terrifyingly *universal* vision with exhaustive youthful zeal.

(R. J. Jarvis)

Earnest archaeologists of 3000 AD guess mistakenly as to the nature of some remnants of our present civilisation:

Evidence of occupation by a warrior caste has been unearthed at the Glasgow site, 'Tam's Bar'. Apart from small, arrow-like weapons, the most interesting find is a metal vessel which we believe may have been used in macabre tests of manhood.

The vessel consists of a bowl disfigured by burn marks and surrounded by a ridge containing four shallow troughs, each just large enough to accommodate a human finger. Those aspiring to warrior status may have been subjected in groups of four to an 'ordeal by fire' with their fingers resting in the troughs as the contents of the bowl were ignited. The inscription *Craven A* on the base of the bowl would have reminded the young Scots that all who flinched were cowards. Perhaps this was the main purpose of the hitherto mysterious festival, Burns Night, and gave rise to the warrior's taunt of 'Get your finger out!'

(Ashtray: Paddy Maher)

The illustration shows an extensible sceptre or wand of clearly shamanistic significance. It was probably carried as a rod of office. When rapidly extended and closed it produces a simple but pleasing music which we can imagine accompanying the chanting of hymns. The brevity of the flexible *flagellum* contained in the hollowed tube and attachable to the reverse end by means of a screw-thread suggests an emblematic rather than a functional scourge (although its metal tip gives rather a nasty laceration). The blatantly phallic design, combined with its ingeniously engineered capacity to grow in length, points to probable use in fertility rites or defloration ceremonies— although experiments suggest that these are likely to have been symbolic rather than orgiastic.

The wand is obviously the repository of diverse magical powers and seems to have been employed by the priest class in conjunction with the two-wheeled prayer frames.

(Bicycle pump: Gerard Benson)

Tape 184. Report begins: The object is round, *circa* 1981, with a segmented exterior, and appears to be some kind of fossilised bromeliaceous fruit. I'm going to try to cut it open . . . no, it doesn't yield to my knife-blade. Now I'm tapping it with a hammer . . . negative. Now I'm dropping it on the floor . . . again negative. Really tough integument—could almost be metal. But I still think it's a fruit, probably *Ananas sativus*. No leaves of course, they would have perished long ago, but there is a ring-shaped appendage at the top which seems to be detachable from the fruit itself . . . yes, I'm removing it now, and it's got this pin-like extension which has come out quite eas

(Hand grenade: Roger Woddis)

Mrs Malaprop guides us round Stonehenge:

This great muniment was construed many years ago in zoological times before the Ancient Bretons and Dudes came to this country. It is designed as a colander to confute the rising and setting of the sun and moon and other celibate bodies at the summer and winter solitudes. The large stones are called multiliths and are sergeants from the Wiltshire downs and the smaller blue ones were brought by human mussels alone from the Priestly Mountains in Wales. All around are other relics of the Beaky people. They buried their chiefs in huge wheel-barrows and tumbrils with many strange celebrations and humane sacrileges which were intended to propinquitate their gods. Recent architectural execrations have revealed a lot about these people, but there are many ancient mistresses waiting still to be absolved.

(John Sweetman)

Paracrostics

the initial letters of the
lines spelling out the first
line

Lipograms

written without use of
the letter *e*

and

Clerihews

whose rhymes are eye-rhymes

Moguls at the BBC
Oppose rude words and blasphemy.
Gory scenes must not be shown,
Undressed persons left alone,
Likewise programmes that suggest
Sinners sometimes come off best.

Alas! when on our screens each night
TV shows are Whitehouse white
The viewers will no longer stay
Home to watch a cleaned-up play.
Elsewhere they'll find (in forms far worse)
Birds who strip and blokes who curse.
BBC men, doubt it not—
Censorship may *start* the rot.
                    (J. M. Crooks)

O gas, do not go off!
Grant still your kindly boon.
Allowing us to scoff
Some well-warmed food at noon.

Despite the striker's blow,
Or militant's decree,
Nitescent be your glow
On kettles filled for tea.

Try still to warm our hearth.
Give ease to frozen toes.
Oh shine, in sunlight's dearth,
On cold-nipped ears and nose!

Flame, phoenix-like at dawning burn,
Frying our breakfast to a turn!
(G. J. Blundell)

A World Cup languor sinks us in our chairs
And Spain transforms our humdrum living-room
As millions manfully dig in downstairs
To watch our lads walk out to instant doom—
Rigid with hooch, spasmodically looking
(Through pupils bloodshot, hollow, moribund)
At Shilton, Robson, Francis, Mills and Brooking,
On whom our wishful fancy pours a fund
Of pity, warmth, nostalgia and good luck.
No trophy is forthcoming, all must know,
But Ron is not a man to pass a buck:
'What counts is putting on a sporting show.'
So what's it all about? Our pundits say
That common signs support a diagnosis—
Victors in lunar orbits chant 'Hurray!'
And losing squads catch chronic psittacosis.
(Basil Ransome-Davies)

Mistral
Around this vivid foam-girt bay
Antiquity casts up its shards,
And music draws a gambolling throng
Of nymphs and satyrs, warriors, bards.
A tropic sun lights up this rout,
Slim sunburnt limbs match tawny sand,
Young goats lock horns in mimic bout
And living glows a classic land.
But southward flows a turbid flood
And loudly roars a chilling blast.
That looming cloud is shot with blood
And throws a shadow, ominous, vast.
Pollution crawls toward this plot,
Consigning all that brightly bloom—
All that sustain our human lot—
Into a common plastic tomb.

'(Jim Holland)

Swiss Miscalculation
From grassy alp right to our barnyard
Our dairy-cows slowly trod down;
Larks rising sang carols, to Lisa
In Swiss national dirndl of brown.

A milkmaid sun-gold is my Lisa,
With rosy lips, moist, soft and warm;
No sylph-slim, slight woodnymph or dryad,
But luscious and buxom of form.

But why did that amorous wind-gust
Swoop out of a bright cobalt sky
On Lisa's light apron and dirndl,
Ballooning both almost waist-high?

For I, all agog at this vision,
On plump charms laid hands, and, poor fool,
In firm arms was caught to soft bosom
And slung in our duckpond to cool.
(Richard Probyn)

I sprawl in lazy fashion
And absorb warm soothing rays,
My couch a bank of smooth-cut turf,
My book Macaulay's *Lays*.

A misty glass is nigh at hand
And, if my throat is dry,
I gulp a draught of icy drink.
'Ah! That was good!' I sigh.

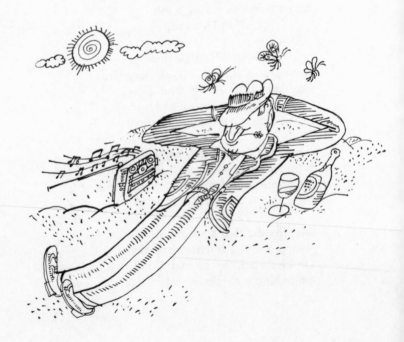

I drop my book. It's much too hot
On such a day as this
For 'I will stand at thy right hand';
Simply to bask is bliss.

But by my watch it's four o'clock.
Just right for BBC!
I flick a switch. Soft bass; now horns—
Brahms' No. 2 in D.
                    (Andrew Hodgson)

Look on this Roman arch half sunk in sand,
Last outpost of Augustan writ and law,
Facing a vast and unknown Asian land,
The hollow symbol of a lion's paw.
No caravans pass by in clouds of dust,
No guardians stand to arms, for in this post
Sharp Roman swords long rotting into rust
And skulls mark havoc by a Mongol host.
Now, in this sun-struck tomb, all things stand still.
Only an aircraft spills its vapour trail
On crystal sky and distant, hazy hill,
Its wings in flight a swiftly moving sail:
A dragon-fly ignoring Roman glory,
Adding its comma to our human story.
                    (Desmond)

If Johann Sebastian Bach
Had remembered to attach
Braces to his levis
He wouldn't have been so embarrassed while conducting a *missa
    brevis*.

                    (Stuart Woods)

François Charles Gounod
Was a highly inventive old bod,
Who wrote many a tuneful aria,
Including the famous 'Ave Maria'.
     (Robert Baird)

Auberon Waugh
Makes some people laugh,
But fewer, I gather,
Than his father.
     (F. Galway)

Debussy
Was terribly fussy.
It took him ages
To compose 'Images'.
     (Joyce Johnson)

Mrs Margaret Thatcher
Has to be a weight-watcher.
In a grocer's daughter
Corpulence is no matter for laughter.
     (John Sweetman)

Business as Unusual

Very ordinary products aimed to sell at a very extraordinary price in the millionaires' market:

Stig is a craggy blond. Each morning he takes his axe into the Scandinavian forests and selects for us a fine, tall pine.

Charmian is our dark-eyed buyer. Her sensitive fingers pick out choicest fibres from a range of exotic and colourful materials. Together with the fruits of Stig's labour, they make something which we feel is rather special.

Derwent is sensitive too. He has received a long apprenticeship in the mysteries of origami. Derwent is proud of that. That's why we like him to design our envelopes.

Stig, Charmian and Derwent have invested a great deal of strength, sensitivity and experience in producing their envelope for you. They call it 'Buff' and think that for only £4.99 a packet you'll be happy to become part of the enriching world of envelopes.

(N. J. Warburton)

We know that you're special. And you know you're special too.
You've got that indefinable something which puts the style into life-style.
You lead a busy life. But even you need to be alone sometimes, to sit and to contemplate. And it's for those quiet moments that we've formulated an essential aid.

From the most perfect trees, specially grown in the towering forests of Sweden, we've created something soft as a whisper, smooth as a kiss, spun fine as a spider's web.

Boxed individually, and available only to holders of gold credit cards, Brømø costs just £10 per pack. And every sheet has the rustle of distinction.

(M. W. Jacob)

The story of civilisation is the story of measurement. But still, how little we know exactly. Just how long is the cork in your bottle of Mouton Rothschild? Or the cord in your Dior pyjamas? Or the Fabergé belt, so elegant about your escort's waist? You need never be in doubt again with our exclusive, fast-becoming-famous *The Tape Measure*.

Woven from selected Egyptian cotton, dyed with gamboge exported from Canton, engraved with measurements originally executed by a Parisian artist in the school of Toulouse-Lautrec, tipped at either end with the finest Swedish steel finished in the fashionable matt style, *The Tape Measure* always sees you right, in good old inches *and* up-to-the-minute centimetres. Our craftsmen began making precision instruments for connoisseurs at the court of King Alonzo III; now our award-winning designers lead in contemporary styling. For this classic, just £24.95.

(J. H. M. Donald)

Short sleeve notes for LPs which, though calculated to satisfy the record company, would warn the potential purchaser not to buy:

Fortissimozart
(played by Jack Orl and his Wolf Gang)
The quintessence of Mozart's Quintets and the pops from his ops have here been extracted and re-orchestrated for guitar, marimba, cymbals, bongos and kettledrum; an unbeatable (or should one say a definitely beatable?) combination, and by some magic fluke our recording technique has produced some absolutely stunning effects.

On the flip side is the Cosy Fantasia, played by the En Bee Gees. Need one say more, other than whether you have these recordings for background music or amplified for your Disco Nachtmusik (Viele rather than Kleine), all Wamjazz buffs will agree that these performances wash the eighteenth century right out of Mozart's hair.

(Joyce Johnson)

Don Giovanni

Moderna is offering this updated version of an old favourite, designed
to appeal to old and young alike.

Traditionalists will respect the majestically slow tempo maintained
throughout, while the interestingly international mix of soloists, some
well known to aficionados for more than a quarter of a century, others
young singers from distant outposts of the operatic world not
previously heard on record, combine excitingly under the iron hand of
the conductor, Hans Lautsprecher, who draws from this hitherto
unknown orchestra a remarkable and sustained volume of sound.

Our younger enthusiasts come into their own with the big burn-up
in the last-act banqueting scene with its raging inferno climax—very
much, we think, their kind of thing in its outburst of violence.

(M. S. Garrett)

Some completely useless Christmas gifts:

Your house keeps you dry! Why not keep your house dry with a
stylish house-jacket? Made from stout polythene, you can choose
traditional red-brick or olde-worlde half-timbered pattern. Sizes:
terrace, semi, detached.

(V. Ernest Cox)

Dirty doormat? Fit a *Protecta* doormat cover.
Guaranteed to keep doormats free from dirt and mud. Woven in
hessian, the cover features a charming portrait of Di and Charles.

(V. Ernest Cox)

Cut your own hair with *Kwickie-Clippie* electric rotary shears.
Periscope attachment and convex mirrors. As used by leading
footballers and TV personalities.

(Desmond)

Telly-screen cloth—in assorted colours and patterns to match any furnishing scheme. Just cover the set whenever you do not wish to view a particular programme.

(Harrison Everard)

For hot summer nights—the easy-to-fill cold-water bottle. Guaranteed to remain cool at least part of the night.

(Edward Samson)

Nix. The noiseless, motionless, invisible toy for the hungover executive.

(I. C. Snell)

Thermally heated dentarium, tastefully decorated in art nouveau or Royal Stuart tartan. Dentures delightfully warm for waking. No more ice-cold gums for Gran!

(George Moor)

Competitors were asked to include eight brand names in a piece of prose:

'There's no need for a fit of the wimpeys, Mrs G, your husband has only got a mild form of aquascutum. A few days in spode and he'll be perfectly oxo. Some tea and toast will keep his horlicks working, and give him a gillette of burgundy if he's down in the dunhills. But chubb the gin and whisky. Two of these omegas last thing will make him sleep, but only two, mind you. He'll want another sandeman for support when reading. Take his bollinger night and morning and ring me if it goes over the twinings. Any questions? Oh, that! Don't worry, my dear, there's nothing wrong with his huntley and palmers.'

(Desmond)

'Take a pifco at this, sarge.' Harris pointed at the bedroom door. Fresh blood trickled down the durex finish paintwork. Sergeant Riley nudged open the door. 'Oh horlicks!' he exclaimed. 'Get an ambulance, schweppes!' Inside, a young woman lay quite persil on

the floor. Riley felt for her pulse. Nothing. 'She's had a right belling round the head—whoever did this must be completely off his skol.' 'Shall I laker the station?' inquired Harris. 'Yes, tell them what we've found, then come back and wait here,' answered Riley. 'I'd rather wait outside,' said Harris, looking vosene. 'This place gives me the ruddles.'

(V. Ernest Cox)

A slightly different Thanksgiving hymn:

Thank Heaven for Michelangelo,
For Bosch, Toulouse-Lautrec, Corot,
Da Vinci, Rembrandt and Monet,
On coffee-tables, on display:

For Science, Literature and Art,
For Shakespeare, Kenneth Clark, Descartes,
Masters and Johnson, Chaucer, Freud.
In paperback for us deployed.

For all that Science doth afford,
Of lowlier sort, we bless the Lord:
Detergents, non-drip paint, TV,
Electric shavers, DDT.

For these too we our thanks impart:
Bach, Beethoven, Brahms, Mozart,
Tchaikovsky, Haydn, Berlioz,
On our hi-fi, in stereo.

For slides, home-movies, plastic macs,
For drip-dry shirts and non-crease slacks,
For plonk and package holidays,
The bounty of the Lord we praise.
(Richard Probyn)

An eccentric poet of the past, William McGonagall, welcomes the New Smoking Material:

Hail, New Smoking Material that has given us the cancer-free
  cigarette,
Or so it is hoped, for it has not been fully tested yet.
It has been very widely advertised, a fact no one can deny,
So that all people have to do is to hurry along and buy.

There have been complaints regarding the New Smoking
   Material's taste
But there are other important facts which also have to be faced:
For tobacco itself does not taste very nice at first
Any more than beer does when first drunk to quench the thirst.
It therefore behoves everybody to try NSM again and again and
   again,
Whether they prefer their cigarettes with filter-tips or plain.
For even the nastiest taste can be got used to if tried often enough,
And so New Smoking Material should not be rejected after just
   one puff.
Socialists, who are so good at forcing people to do things they do
   not like,
Should ban all real tobacco, even though some people might
   strike.
After all, if people found that they were still spitting and
   choking,
They could always stop by merely giving up smoking.
                              (E. O. Parrott)

Some new products named after Shakespearian characters:

Do *your* walls have ears? Ensure privacy in the home by installing
Polonius tapestry curtains interwoven with electronic filaments
possessing highly sensitive acoustic properties. Instant warning of
eavesdroppers and interlopers is guaranteed. Proof against moles and
rodents. Washing with soft soap and distilled water removes the
darkest stains. As used in the Kremlin, White House, Quai d'Orsay,
Swiss banks, Interpol, Buckingham Palace, and Number Ten,
Downing Street. All orders handled in strict confidence and fitted by
certified Danish craftsmen.

                       (Desmond)

Ask your tailor. The elegant world is at last returning to the
button—and the *Lear Button* in particular—after the long infamous
reign of the unreliable zip. 'Pray you undo this button'—a cry for help

from the aged Lear—is a reassurance to all those who have experienced the zip which will not close before joining the ladies at the end of an important dinner party. The *Lear Button* is fashioned to hold tight in all circumstances.

(G. Greene)

Pretentious wine blurbs:

This inexpensive white Scheiss is too important to permit insincerity; it is true as time itself, deepening in tone with age with an ethereal bouquet reminiscent of the unsophisticated vintages of Arschloch. Tight-cheeked and appropriate for delicate fish dishes, it goes well with baked barracuda. The 69er, bottled by Furz and Pinkeln from the vines in the famous Gettingemschloscht region, is by far the best buy. It has a maturity that has lost its angularity without acquiring the flaccidity of the more senile vintages. Do sample this rare wine 'cooled a long age in the deep-delvèd earth', or, in this case, in the cellars of the Bummel. Available now in all supermarkets.

(P. W. R. Foot)

Hitherto synthetic wine could be robust—never svelte. Here's one I can recommend as actually better than the natural variety, for it is silky as well as powerful, has a soft edge, large-scale yet graceful, and is both fastidious and charming.

Halcyon Harvest 1980 has an aristocratic languor with the bouquet of a great wine possessing real substance. The chemists have wrought a miracle. Free of any sulkiness or vulgarity despite its provenance, this is a true wine whose insinuating first taste has sinewy elegance and a heroic finish. Here is a classic vintage of great depth—its first taste is a minuet, its after-taste a symphony. Need one say more?

(T. Griffiths)

Imaginary government advertisements bravely attempt to attract recruits to unappealing jobs:

Owing to the premature death of the previous incumbent a vacancy, has arisen for a wardress at the Toxteth Progressive Prison for violent female offenders.

The successful applicant will work as a team leader and will live on equal terms with the inmates, sharing sleeping accommodation and prison duties to foster an atmosphere of concern and involvement. She will take groups of twenty women on rehabilitation visits to local shops, banks and public houses to test the success of our reform programme, and will at all times be responsible for their behaviour.

An important aspect of the job will be the monthly progress report which is delivered in person to the local Monday Club.

The salary is more generous than it appears when the free uniform and accommodation are taken into account. A pension scheme is inappropriate but good dependants' benefits are paid.

(Sheelagh Panton)

A bright, alert, able school-leaver (one CSE) is required in the Bootle Regional Headquarters of the Inland Revenue to assist with the smooth operation of the internal communications system.

Duties comprise the efficient running of the recently-installed modern office Lift, with its well-lighted and airy lift-cage, capacity 1000 lb (six persons), with easy-to-operate control panel and attractive decor, which interconnects the basement (canteen) area with ground (PAYE), first and second (VAT) and third floor (coding) departments.

The post promises both mobility and independence, with scope for interesting face-to-face social involvement relating to all grades from secretarial and supervisory to executive staff. There are opportunities to exercise mechanical skills calling for a degree of precision, offering responsibility and job-satisfaction. You will be part of a successful, well-motivated team as an operative (Grade III). Attractive uniform provided.

(Ron Jowker)

And, Oh!
'Tis Delicious to
Hate You!

A purchase at the sales is lamented:

> I bought this jacket in the Sale,
> Belinda says it's made of sacking
> And makes my cheeks look ghastly pale.
> I bought this jacket in the Sale,
> Look how it billows in the gale.
> Will someone tell me, What *is* hacking?
> I bought this jacket in the Sale,
> Belinda says it's made of sacking.
>   (John Sweetman)

Curses in poetic form prompted by someone providing bad service:

> Accursed the counter-girl who chatters,
> Keeps you waiting while she natters
> Of fabled youths called Wayne or Ed,
> And which of them is tops in bed,
> And so-and-so's engagement ring,
> And how she dreamt last night of Sting,
> Then, when you venture to address
> Her, flays you with a testy '*Yes?*'
> Oh may the bitch receive her dues
> By standing evermore in queues
> In supermarkets—then have posed
> In front of her: '*This Checkout Closed*'.

Dead prematurely, may St Peter
At heaven's very portal mete her
Retribution—make her wait
A billion years outside his gate.
　　　　(Jonathan Fernside)

Take him, O Lord, from the counter
Where he lounges with insolent ease,
And if his responses are languid
Inflict on him arthritic knees.

Take him, O Lord, from the kitchen
Whence he shouts in a hectoring voice,
'This is your lot, so be glad what you've got.'
Let him die of an agonised choice.

Take her, O Lord, from the cash queue
Where her friends are allowed to go past.
Convey them all straight up to Heaven
But explain that the first shall be last.

Take him, O Lord, from the Gas Board
Where he acts as a hot-water-spoiler.
Dispatch him directly to Hell, Lord,
And require him to service their boiler.
                              (J. H. M. Donald)

Blake haunts these desperate verses to a road-drill:

Road drill, road drill, I repeat,
On the surface of the street,
What immoral hand or eye
Could frame thy fearful symmetry?

And what shoulder and what art
Designed the knob that made thee start?
And when thy heart began to beat
What dread hand and what dread feet?

What the vandal, quite insane,
Planned thy hammering with his brain?
What the deafness? What dread clasp
Dare its noisy terrors grasp?

When the man throws down his drill
And stops the rattling of my sill,
Does he smile his work to see—
The broken road as crazed as me?
(T. Griffiths)

Songs against shopkeepers:

When butchers close, though faint with hunger,
I never go to the Fishmonger
But falter on his noisome threshold
Where every prospect turns my flesh cold.
As cold his heart. His ways are gruesome,
He has no pity in his bosom
For trawler-men, their toil and daring;
He nonchalantly splits the herring
And hacks the cod in careless pieces.
Their steaming roe (anaemic faeces)
Lies by pathetic heaps of whitebait
And tasteless parcelled kippers (lightweight).
False lemons sit on his deep-freezer,
Too pale his chips, too green his peas are;
Smirking, with coarse red hands and damp he
Offers stale chicken-legs and scampi.
Skin, bone and gut—he loves to chuck it
Under his sink in a foul bucket
Which, I suspect (the flavour lingers),
He strains to mix up his fish-fingers.
Glimpsing his sly obsequious face
Some day I'll shout, 'Just keep your plaice—
Your prices, like your fish, are high!'
And hold my nose and hurry by.
(P. M.)

His shining apples by the score
With rosy cheeks enchant mine eyes,
I'd swear they're fresh from Ceres' store,
So round, so smooth, so fair a prize.
With eagerness I can't disguise
I pay my money, but alack!
The ones I get are half the size—
He always takes them from the back.

How large and succulently lush
The strawberries that his punnets hold;
His plums and cherries bloom and blush,
His oranges are hugely gold
With beauty that can scarce be told;
But when my purchase I unpack,
They're sour, or rotten, wizened, old—
He always takes them from the back.

It matters not how keen my sight,
However much I'm on my guard,
The stuff I get has grubs, or blight,
The greens are limp, the peas are hard,
The apples scabbed, the pears all scarred.
Why must I satisfaction lack?
Greengrocery my life has marred—
He *always* takes mine from the back.
(W. F. N. Watson)

'These I have loathed':

Milk known as 'long-life' that instantly curdles,
Women in hot-pants who should be in girdles,
Guests who come early and ask if they're late—
These are a few of the things that I hate;

Yesterday's sandwiches, cardboard, pathetic,
Chemical beer that is tasteless, synthetic,
Somebody's lipstick still smearing the glass—
Pubs are becoming a pain in the arse;

Hamburgers, hotdogs, Kentucky fried chicken,
Warm Coca-cola (a substance to sicken),
Tea made from tea-bags and greasy french fries—
These are some more of the things I despise.

Weather forecasters, those glum isobarists,
Disc-jockeys, pop-stars, demented guitarists
Featured on Wonderful Radio One,
Frequently tempt me to purchase a gun;

'Genuine leather' that proves to be plastic,
Government promises (very elastic) . . .
Life becomes harder and harder to face—
Mostly I loathe the entire human race.
                    (Brian Allgar)

Change and Decay in All Around I See

Deviant members of society redefined:

Call-girl: a lay-buy
French batsman: Jacques in a box
(Adam Khan)

Racecourse tipster: public investment counsellor
(J. J. Brownjohn)

Prostitute: a Merchant of Venus
(T. A. Dyer)

Muggers: nut-cracker suite
(P.M.)

Pickpocket: freelance economic adjustor
(Ian Kelso)

What would Rudyard Kipling make of the world today?

The Islanders, 1972
Ye are more—and less—than my People,
since the day that I went to the tomb.
Ye teem in your foetid millions, though ye
butcher the babe in the womb.

The winds of the world have answered: the
  oceans have borne your retreat:
And the yelpers who scorn the English flag,
  now they live in an English street.
Now your leaders proffer your remnants to
  the French and the Hun and the Dutch,
And the Hubshi installed in your cities
  does the work it demeans you to touch;
And your mechanised fields stand silent,
  with your birds choked by chemical tilth,
While ye fill the seas of England with your
  ships'—and your people's—filth;
And your oil and your waste and your
  poison and your ordure cake your beach,
And no child can sleep in your islands for
  your aircraft's maniac screech;
And your churches stand empty and
  crumble—the Spirit within them is dead—
And your 'muddied oafs' in their greatness
  are granted the worship instead;
And your living-room shows ye, in colour,
  the bullet sent, live, through the nape;
And ye queue in the rain to watch incest
  and a 'deeply significant rape';
And 'nation speaks peace unto nation' in a
  mindless and grammarless mutter.
Ye had to abandon an Empire. Did ye have
  to descend to the gutter?
                    (Ronald Balaam)

*Competitors were asked for a poetic preview of the day when the
world's petroleum resources finally run out:*

  (with a bow to Walter de la Mare)
  'Is there anybody there?' said the Traveller,
  And he gave the glass door a great thump,

While the last Morris 8 in existence
Chugged by the leaf-fringed pump.
Then a bird flew up out of a water-can
And the Traveller peered through the door
At the coils of a Green Shield stamp machine
Which had died on its side on the floor.
But no one appeared for the Traveller;
No head poked from under a car
Wiping the grease from its whiskers
And brandishing spanner or spar.
So only the phantom listeners
In the overalls of the dead
Heard that last sad crank of the engine.
'I shall have to walk,' he said.

(Reginald Watters)

*Two sonnets stressing the scenic degeneration that has occurred since
Wordsworth wrote 'Composed on Westminster Bridge':*

Earth has not anything to show more fair
To bland accountants' eyes than this array
Of high monstrosities, this gross display
Of ferro-concrete brutishness. How dare
They with such patent outrage crowd the air?
Where Mammon rules, developers make hay:
For them not 'Does it please?' but 'Does it pay?'
Is obviously the overriding care.
St Paul's is pygmied, the grand scheme designed
By peerless Wren quite overborne. But while
These buildings come from Brobdingnag, the mind
Behind them hails from Lilliput: the scale
Inept, the style inert, the finish vile.
Where Disproportion reigns, all things must fail.

(Andrew McEvoy)

Behold this city which so long defied
Assaults by plague and fire and envious foe,
Now by its self-inflicted wounds brought low
And left with rags and crumbs of ancient pride.
See how the tainted river spews its tide
Past stagnant pools where merchant fleets once lay,
While concrete jungles seal the slow decay
Of palaces and spires whose lease has died.
Within these ivory towers new slums are born
Where strangers live so near, yet far apart.
No joyful chorus greets the smiling morn,
No genial warmth revives the city's heart.
So if the child be father to the man,
The clock runs back to where the race began.

(Desmond)

*Two up-to-date demons, Speed and Television, are described by a
modern Milton and Bunyan:*

First Speed, a monstrous demon, dripping blood
Of little children and of aged folk
Whose cries unto the bar of heav'n ascend
Inutile. Him men worship near and far.
His face essential evil manifests;
Huge blazing eyes his savage nature flaunt
And through his grinning lips sharp, hungry teeth
Imply their horrid purposes at large.
When man from home emerges and ascends
His carriage automotive, to proceed
Upon a journey and assumes control,
Straightway the demon mounts upon his back
And calls upon him for his worship due.
Th' impellent pedal man will then depress,
And sacrifices, hapless young and old,
Thick as autumnal leaves will strew the way.

(H. A. C. Evans)

Then said my Lord Do Nought unto Christian, Thou hast spoken much to me of the Demons thou hast overcome, but I will show thee one who is of good intent, and a right merry Devil withal, whose delight it is to entertain poor wayfarers.

And he took Christian into the house of my Lord Pass Time, where this Devil had his abode; and the name of the Devil was Television. And he had on a glittering breast-plate, wherein were to be seen, as in a mirror, all the shows and pomps and vanities of this wicked world. Whereupon Christian, beholding his companions worshipping Television, said unto himself, I see that this Devil inviteth but to sloth and wantonness of the eye! Then, seizing his staff, he departed, and sought the road whereby he thought he might come to a view of the Delectable Mountains.

(G. J. Blundell)

Shaw and Sheridan comment on the National Theatre:

You can always tell a good theatre by the vulgarity of its interior. The good ones have plenty of red velvet and gilded cherubs: the bad ones, concrete. These days a designer thinks he is aesthetic only when he is uncomfortable. All good theatres are a theatrical experience before the curtain rises. The National Theatre is not a playhouse, it's a machine from the Bauhaus. Good architecture? You don't expect me to know who the architect is, do you? If it's by a good architect, it's good architecture, naturally. That stands to reason. Denis Lasdun? Never heard of him.

(T. Griffiths)

Sneer: The National Theatre, in proper hands, might certainly be made the school of entertainment; but now, I am sorry to say it, people seem to go there principally for their morality.
Dangle: Egad, I think the worst alteration is in the common appearance of the audience. No dinner jackets, no evening dresses; even Her Majesty, were she ever to attend (which is unlikely, unless the play be *Equus*), would not be admitted, were she not attired in jeans and T-shirt.

(138)

Sneer: I doubt she would attend the present production. It is called *How's Your Belly Off for Spots?*
Dangle: What is its purpose?
Sneer: To make the stage a hospital that treats social diseases.
Dangle: Egad, it sounds truly entertaining.

(Roger Woddis)

Great names from the past provide comments on listening to a House of Commons broadcast for the first time:

The Duke of Wellington

I had thought our own cohorts of Jacobins, ideologues, and careerists as sorry a company as one could withstand, but today's House of Commons has the additional imposition of boredom. To hear the ignorant on a rostrum is to plumb the depths of ennui, such as I had not felt since the Peninsula. What is deplorable is that such sorry creatures dub themselves men of action and use military phraseology like homely Hectors: 'The spirit of Dunkirk', 'Backs to the wall', 'The battle for the pound', and all the rest of it. Surely it is enough for these jackasses to bray without trying to prance? Damme. I am not surprised to hear the place is full of vegetarians, pacificators, sellers of nostrums and hawkers of consciences. They look like that, they sound like that, and by God they smell like that. The Devil take them, and soon.

(J. J. Crown)

Bernard Shaw

It was not so much a Heartbreak as a Ribs-Ache House. I cannot recalling laughing so heartily since I last saw *Lear*. Was it possible, I asked myself, that millions of my fellow-citizens had plodded dutifully to their polling-stations, made their marks and elected to represent them such an assembly of braying, self-centred, imbecilic buffoons in the fond belief that they were thereby contributing to the Democratic Process? It would be a farce were it not also a tragedy. A country that produced such giants as Bunyan, Blake, Hogarth, Turner and Morris was capable also of filling the chamber of the Mother of Parliaments with half-witted children. It is beyond belief; and yet I heard with my own ears the chatter of these children, no more concerned with the approaching storm than is a cow-pat in a trampled field. England deserves a better fate.

(Roger Woddis)

British Rail intends to rebuild most of London's rail termini. Here is Sir John Betjeman's reaction:

> Gone the London and North-Eastern,
> London, Brighton and South Coast;
> LMS, Great Western, Southern,
> Names the Railways once could boast:
> Dead the great steam locomotives,
> British Rail is but a ghost.
>
> Now environmental planners
> Eye the London stations too;
> King's Cross, Charing Cross, St Pancras,
> Paddington and Waterloo,
> And in place of Neo-Classic,
> Perpendicular Yahoo.
>
> Farewell, London Bridge and Euston,
> Holborn Viaduct, goodbye;
> High-rise blocks will hide your stations,
> Ugly boxes, gaunt and high;
> Crude successors to the glories
> Of the London Termini.

(W. F. N. Watson)

Travel—Ruin of All Happiness

A sonnet containing a goodly sprinkling of those foreign phrases we find scattered through passages of pretentious prose:

Tempus edax rerum

Rien ne va plus! Well, *che sarà sarà.*
My lot is *dolce far niente,* so
A *nos moutons: mutantur tempora—*
Let others take the stage. That's *comme il faut.*
Non omnia possumus omnes (honi soit
Qui mal y pense): *j'y suis, j'y reste*—that's that!
For me its's *plus ça change;* if *après moi*
Le déluge meets the case I'll eat my hat.
Si non è vero è ben trovato? Well,
Humanum est errare. Sauve qui peut
Is no *modus vivendi.* If it were
(*Experto crede!*), life's a living hell.
Lasciate ogni speranza? Wie so stumm?
Dum spiro spero. Cogito ergo sum.
                    (D. L. L. Clarke)

Public notices in mangled English, such as might be displayed in some foreign country:

The Manager is regrettable that morning service is not held in bedrooms because of little calling for it.

Breakfast (7.00–9.00) is independently organised by the guests from the meets, cripsrolls, and local big cheeses lying in state in the Dining Room. Toasted bread only if begged for specially.

Because of the small size of the waiters lunch must be searched for elsewhere.

Dinner (20.00–22.00) if convenient has a constantly evolving menu to the taste of all prices.

The Manager hope you will stay pleasant and if fire happens will remember not to smoke in bedrooms please.

(J. Timson)

The governance of this natural monstrosity is adverting to the peoples adventurous upon the entrails of this notorious chasm that it is not possessing itself of responsibility, in especial to those incident to nervosity, vertiginals, or the fitful convulsions, for damages consequent upon the phenomenal droppings of limestone moistures or any other derangements to their persons or vestures during the visitations. The peoples wishful of embarking the vessels for the penetration of the uttermost grottoes are respectively chided that they must subjugate themselves to the desires of their boatmen with the most expeditious immediacy.

(Martin Fagg)

Please to propel all boats of rowing discreetly, advancing with sameness of direction by arrows indicating; thus collidings will not enjoy prevalence, and drowning mortality will become negligent.

Exchanging of persons' seats, and erections on the foots, are impressively forbidden; likewise of horse-playing and larking in the sky.

Navigators must tenaciously adhere to the printed table of times.

At the whistle's blowing, boaters must deposit their skulls, and take no further proceedings.

(Pascoe Polglaze)

Kindly do not take advantages of these conveniences whilst you are standing still in the railway station. Flushes are only allowable while your train is moved between stations.

The seating is raised in certain circumstances understood by them.

Do not carpet the flooring with paper towels but put yourself in the bin beside the toilet.

Do not open the window and throw your head out of it.

We regret there is no point for shavings in here.

(B. Mooring)

If you are being dirty in the bathroom and are in crying need of extra soapings and towellings, take advantage of the servicewoman. She is lying in waiting for your convenience. The servicewoman is at all moments very trying, but it assists in her servicing if you are leaving the bathroom and etsetera as you were on entering.

(I. C. Snell)

A new national anthem for Australia:

> Arise, arise, Australia!
> May your billabongs not fail yer!
>   May you never lose
>   Your dinkum booze
> That makes your males much maler.
>
> Salute, salute, Australia!
> Let no enemy assail yer!
>   And tell those poms
>   And Chinky Coms
> They'll get bashed unless they hail yer!
>
> Fly, flag of great Australia,
> As to the mast we nail yer!
>   You'll win each game
>   While Barry's Dame
> With praises does regale yer!
>
> (E. O. Parrott)

Competitors were asked for a poem describing the characteristics of a nation they had never been able to warm to:

> Who starts an argument when no one else
>   would care a jot?
> Who keeps on quarrelling for reasons he has
>   long forgot?

Who joins a fight before he knows who's
    fighting who for what?
The Scot.

Who wakes with trembling hand and eye
    bloodshot?
Who brags that he can always drink another
    tot?
Who afterwards falls down and then brings up
    the lot?
The Scot.

Who, if he loses a football match, calls it a
    plot?
Who doesn't change his underwear but lets it
    rot?
Who wears a paste-brush on his groin to
    advertise what underneath he hasn't got?
The Scot.
        (J. H. M. Donald)

      One deeply detests
      Those queer folk who dine
      On ancient birds' nests
      And (just think!) rice wine.

      Far worse, when they eat
      They do juggling tricks
      With pieces of meat
      Upon two thin sticks.

      It's custom, they say.
      Well, they can stick it!
      Chinks can't even play
      The game of cricket.
         (Edward Samson)

An extract from publicity material advertising the South Coast, or, as the BMJ calls it, the Costa Geriatrica:

We are smart operators in the touristic trade. Spanish Fly is dealing of yore with travel to Spain, but we are now content to offer many pleasurable openings to esteemed dotards in Britain. We invite you to attend our journeys to your own stunning ressorts for a flawless recess.

Come to suny Bournemout for a really swingeing time! Regard what beckons you at the Hotel Methusela!

We hang down below some of the attractive draws for senor citizens:

*Well-grounded nurses at hand to comfort your wants.

*Special rates for ladies and gentlemen in their second childhood.

*Hot water in each room.

*Bathe-chairs for those who are rocky on their pins.

*A game room where guests may disport themselves at bingo, serpents and ladders or whatsoever tickles their fancy.

Write now for our lurid booklet—we can promise a hot summer for has-beens!

(Roger Woddis)

A poem whose rhymes consist of words pronounced alike but with different meanings, on the subject of holidays:

> To holiday at home I'm fain,
> No foreign lingo can I feign.
> Down with Abroad: let Britain reign
> In spite of strikes and fog and rain;
> Her rural cot and rustic wain
> Arouse a love that n'er shall wane.
> To tour abroad I would not deign,
> Gaping at Dutchman, Swede and Dane,
> And who would choose, were he quite sane,
> To leave the Thames for Rhine or Seine,
> Nor would I want to rush by plane

O'er sea and river, hill and plain;
I vow 'twould give me but a pain
Glimpsed thus through cabin window pane.
But there, too long is my refrain—
So from more lines I now refrain.
(Tom Brewer)

*'Hastings: Popular with visitors since 1066'—Competitors were
asked for similar slogans for Great Britain's resorts and towns:*

BAKEWELL: For tarts with a difference.
BATH: We need no plug.
PLYMOUTH: All nationalities welcome—even Spaniards.
LIVERPOOL: Our Sound's unique.
(P. W. R. Foot)

WIGAN: Has no peer.
DOVER: Where English customs can be seen at their best.
(Paul Griffin)

ABERDEEN: Where you can save money while on holiday.
(John Sweetman)

You shouldn't miss Skipton Castle—Cromwell didn't.
(J. Timson)

CREWE: Come here for a change.
(Betsy Lee)

Reflections while waiting for a bus:

Bus Fever (with a bow to John Masefield)
I must down on my knees again, by the lonely stop in the High,
And all I ask is a 78 and a trip to Peckham Rye,

And the heel's kick and the bell's ping and my raised hand's
    shaking,
And a grey sludge on the road's face and the driver braking.

I must down on my knees again, for the hope of an easy ride
Is a vain hope, and it's odds-on I'll have to stand inside;
And all I ask is a half-filled bus and the pavements drying,
And a young bird on the next seat, and a baby crying.

I must down on my knees again, for I've stood here half my life,
And it won't be so surprising if I run amok with a knife!
For all I ask is the chance to use my laughable Red Bus Rover,
And quiet sleep on the top deck when the long wait's over.
                                        (Roger Woddis)

*Honesty subtly combines with tact when competitors are invited to
comment on friends' holiday slides and snaps:*

Ah, in this one I see you have succeeded quite brilliantly in
emphasising the Italianate influence in Wilton Church architecture, by
giving that marvellously artistic slant to the campanile, which
instantly brings Pisa to mind . . .

   Now there's another really impressive study, Henry! What I find so
exciting is the masterly way in which you've obtained this romantic,
misty blurring, as though seen through tears—so utterly *right* for a
gentle pastoral subject of patient cows in muddy pastures; yet how
amusing to have captured the rump of one in close-up as your
foreground . . .

   And how delightfully, extraordinarily clever, to have controlled the
lighting in this so skilfully that your wife's resemblance to her talented
grandmother is so dramatically and unmistakably evoked . . .
                                        (William Hodson)

Dear Gladys,
   Thank you ever so for the wedding photos Jim took. What a nice
one of the bride in her white. Fred wondered if she is expecting or if it

was the wind blowing her dress. Grands thought it was a polar bear at the zoo, but her sight is fading, poor dear. Whose bald head was it above Mildred's hat in the family group? Her Harold hasn't come back, surely? Is it that Percy Hucklebuck, ashamed to show his face? What a pretty little thing Sonia has become, even though she had to stick her face round Charlie's legs. The spitting image of her cousin Shirley. I suppose there was nothing in those rumours. Yes, the bridegroom looks a strapping fellow. I'm sure they had a lovely honeymoon.

(Stephen Meadows)

How very interesting. Were you consciously influenced by being in France—the home of the moderns? You weren't? Then it must have been your subconscious. Take this one of Mary in the Park. One sees that shadowy, almost out-of-focus effect in so many of Seurat's paintings. And then this one of baby John on the beach. You get everything sharply defined and snap it just as he holds the beachball in front of his face. One gets the impression of a baby with a beachball for a head. Pure Magritte. And the third one, the close-up of the baby where he hides everything but his left leg behind the big breakfast food carton. It's almost as though Salvador Dali had collaborated with Andy Warhol.

(Kate Short)

Some highly unlikely 'paradises' as advertised by travel brochures:

Why not take a self-catering holiday at Inchcape this year? Situated 12 miles south-east of Arbroath in the fairway of vessels making for the Tay and the Forth, the fully detached accommodation is out of this world, being a penthouse prototype of the high-rise flat. Designed by Robert Stevenson, grandfather of R.L., it was a favourite retreat of Sir Ralph McSouthey, a founder of the Rover Scouts. The lounge windows give excellent views of the Angus coast and the Grampian mountains and make an ideal observation post for shipping and birdwatching. The rock runs down to the sea and fishing is free. There are numerous wrecks to explore within easy reach and at high tide you can relax in the soothing waters of the North Sea, which comes right up to your front door. A resident janitor is willing to undertake light duties.

(John Bennett)

See Labrador and die! Spend an exhilarating break at Hammertoe-fröst Summit Lodge where Erik the Raw landed 900 years ago! Fine exposure walks. Round-of-peaks nature trail. Canoeing and swimming. Ample self-reliance opportunities. Genuine Eskimo cuisine—the varieties of blubber will astonish you! Evening games—dirt stove musical chairs, hunt the blanket etc. Beds regularly sprinkled for your greater comfort. Guests met at foot of massif and guided personally to Lodge.

Approved by Labrador Chamber of Commerce. Six months' supplies always held.

(B. Simpson)

Have you ever longed to leave the 'civilised' world and escape to a distant shore where only the lapping waters which fringe the palm-studded shore break the silence of a tropical paradise? Now Guinea Coasters Ltd embark at Dogura, New Guinea, and leave you to experience the challenges and delights of primitive life.

Merge with the missionaries and learn how to cook on a wood-fired stove, to shampoo from a watering-can or to barter with natives for pumpkin tops, or for limes with monks who live over the hill.

No matter when you arrive, the summery temperature of Dogura will compel you to take it easy! Explore the nearby jungle (head-hunters are at least thirty miles distant), swim in the coral-bedded turquoise sea or simply relax under your mosquito net. Book now with Guinea Coasters and experience life amongst a freshly independent nation.

(Lettice Buxton)

Enthusiastic holiday reports calculated to chill the spine of a stay-at-home:

> Stretch A7,
> The Bog of Allen,
> Co. Westmeath,
> Ireland.

You simply must drop everything and join us here. The nearest station is Mullingar, only nineteen miles. We're planting trees on a stretch of reclaimed bog. There are twenty-four of us (all nationalities) and we aim to plant between 750 and 1000 trees per head every day—slightly less when it's wet. We live simply, in small tents on the bog. The other evening a few of the tents (including ours) were blown away, but we caught up with them eventually. A thoroughly invigorating life. We get provisions from a sort of mobile canteen which calls once a week. It also brings us post and papers. Just think: the nearest place is eight miles and I believe that if needed a doctor has to be helicoptered!

> (James Comyn)

Dear Mother,

Arrived on Sunday at 12. Slept in the lay-by at the turn off to Dorchester—slept in the same one now for thirty years! While waiting to get in flat, booked it again for next year. We cleaned it out. Had taken a new scrubbing brush as usual. Down to the beach. Had to get nasty with a woman with big glasses who wanted to use beach hut number six near the Chippy. Said to her we've had this one for twenty-five years. Booked the beach hut for next year. Had tea. Washed up in new bowl I'd brought with me. All the same old crowd there. It's grand to have a change. Ruby.

> (R. J. Green)

Dear Maud,

I must tell you about our first day at Poets' Farm. It is marvellously exhilarating and such an intellectual stimulus; one feels a new awareness of the inscapes of Nature. We begin with meditation—two perfectly blissful silent hours—then breakfast, lemon juice and rye bread, so basic.

This morning the Master read a perfect haiku of his own and explained its meaning on the first three levels of understanding. He will expound the higher levels when we are purified—probably on Friday.

Before I wrote this I did my theme for tomorrow. We were given a sonnet and told to express the inner essence in seven syllables! Mine is, 'Fallen image in sand, Woe!' . . .

(John Sweetman)

A brief address to Melancholy occasioned by train travel:

> Will the 8.20 take me all the way?
>   Yes, and round the bend.
> And how long is the journey, would you say?
>   From morn to night, my friend.
> And are there light refreshments on the train?
>   Refreshments? That's a laugh.
> And once I'm there, will I get back again?
>   God, no, they're short of staff.
> Shall I be seated? Will the signals fail?
>   A seat? You won't get in.
> How are they packed who go by British Rail?
>   Like sardines in a tin.
> Do they reduce the service at the peak?
>   You're lucky if they run.
> And will it be the same again next week?
>   Too bloody true, old son.

(Roger Woddis)

Reductions
on a Grand Scale

A short verse biography:

> Thus to begin:
> Eleanor Gwyn;
> Born Drury Lane;
> In plays by Behn;
> Talent was reckoned
> By Charles II;
> Bore him a son;
> Got lots of mon.;
> Painted by Lely
> (Posed very freely);
> Caused a furore,
> 'Protestant Whore!';
> Famed for her wit;
> Died in a fit,
> Aged 37.
> Then went to heaven.
> (Gerard Benson)

A Tale of Two Cities

The Knitters are knitting two cities!—
A prisoner everyone pities
  Is reclaimed by his daughter
  And borne o'er the water
Which echoes with bloodthirsty ditties.

An *émigré-aristo* dandy,
Soi-disant Charles Darnay, is handy,
So she can't set her heart on
Our poor bourgeois Carton
Who drudges on second-rate brandy.

Her husband, whose *château* is rubble,
By *bâteau* goes back and meets trouble,
But Carton—how strange—
Gives his head in exchange:
So it's *everyone else* who sees double!
(Gina Berkeley)

A mnemonic of the wives of Henry VIII:

Catherine of Aragon—
Hard-done-by paragon;
Bold Anne Boleyn—
Caught out in sin;
Would there might be more
Of charming Jane Seymour!
Coarse Anne of Cleves'
Horsiness peeves;
Cute Catherine Howard
Was rumbled and Towered;
Which left Catherine Parr
To say, 'Harry, ta-ta!'

Three produced kids;
Two lost their lids;
Two got the chuck;
One had the luck.
(Mary Holtby)

Some celebrated poems barbarously boiled down:

The Lady of Shalott
Saw knight pass
In glass,
Left room,
Full of gloom,
Stole boat,
Died afloat.
(Fiona Pitt-Kethley)

Lycidas
College mate
Lost at sea;
Could same fate
Lurk for me?
Would have been
Perfect pastor;
present scene
Sheer disaster.
Don't cry; he's OK.
Got my coat; on my way.
(O. Smith)

The Ancient Mariner
Old salt
Grabs third,
Tells what
Once occurred.
His fault:
'Shot bird,
Saw ghost,
Crew die,
Ship lost,
Not I.'
(John Stanley)

The Solitary Reaper
Up hill creeping
Saw her reaping,
Singing, bending.
Song heart-rending.
What? Cannot say;
But lovely lay!
(P. W. R. Foot)

The Listeners
'Who's at home?' Traveller knocks.
Bangs again. Violent shocks
Wake the ghosts. Phantom hosts
Hear the din. No one in.
Final whack. Calls, 'I'm back.
Had to try.' No reply.
Gallops down lanes.
Silence reigns.
(Jean Hayes)

Anno Domini

Definitions of getting old:

You don't notice the smell any more when the toast burns.
(Ron Jowker)

You're wearing narrow trousers for the second time.
Your wife believes your excuses for getting home late.
(Basil Ransome-Davies)

You can remember people whistling on their way to work.
(Ted Thompson)

Your children no longer bother to argue with you.
(Lawrence Rickard)

Your grandchildren allow you to sit by the window in the bus.
(N. E. Soret)

You start taking moderation to excess.
(Pascoe Polglaze)

You stop loving snow and sweet-corn.
(Susan H. Llewellyn)

You hear the phone ring and hope it's not for you.
(M. G. Cormack)

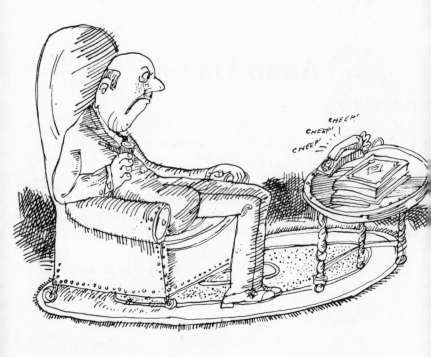

Two sonnets bemoaning lighter physical handicaps:

O Torticollis, Anarch of the Night,
Father of Doom, from chill Arthritis bred,
Blight not this living-room, this bath, this bed,
This little hearth of laughter, warmth and light:
Give me the solace of a short respite
Before I fight thy aftermath of dread,
Render me dumb, or deaf, or daft instead—
But let my head still turn from left to right!

(158)

In vain. The dawn grows pale with shuddering strain,
The harsh alarm-clock shrills again—and hark!
My neck, the Ark of this immortal brain,
Crackles with stiff-packed straw upon the rack
Of sunrise, roars with pain—and sideways, back,
A rudderless wreck steers off into the dark . . .
(Gina Berkeley)

When I consider how my head is bald,
How what was once a rich, luxuriant crop
Of hair has vanished from my thinning top
Till, staring at the mirror, I'm appalled;
When I reflect how madly I'm enthralled
By a girl's tresses as they loosely drop
About her neck, so that I have to stop
And wonder why I had to be so mauled
By nature, my self-confidence is lost.
I'd like to wear a wig, but lack the nerve
To face the smirks of everyone I pass:
Such artificial aids could only serve
To make me feel an even bigger ass—
So between two embarrassments I'm tossed.
(A. J. Ryder)

Competitors were asked for verses suitable for inclusion in When We
Are Very Old *or* Now We Are Eighty-Six:

Christopher Robin is drawing his pension;
    He lives in a villa in Spain;
He suffers from chronic bronchitis and tension,
    And *never* goes out in the rain.

He never wears wellies; he *has* to eat jellies;
    He peers through a pair of bifocals;
He talks quite a lot to a bear that he's got
    Who is known as El Pu to the locals.

Christopher Robin goes cougherty cougherty
    Cougherty cougherty cough;
All sorts and conditions of Spanish physicians
    Have seen him and written him off.

But drowsily still in his house near Seville
    He dreams of the Forest, and Anne,
Who waits in the buttercups—deep in the buttercups
    Down by the stream—for her man.
                    (Paul Griffin)

('*Christopher Robin is saying his prayers*')
Weary old dears, near the end of our day,
Hairless and toothless we mumble away—
Blurred and sclerotic, our muddled old brains
Repeating the same old befuddled refrains,
Bitchy old beldame, weak on her pins,
Stubbing her toes and abrading her shins—
Hush, hush, snigger who dares—
Old Granny Robin has fallen downstairs!
Tetchy and torpid, our limbs in decay,
We fumble and grumble our way through the day:
Study us carefully if you'd behold
The infinite graces your years will unfold.
Garrulous gaffer, ever a curse—
Now, in his dotage, he's twenty times worse.
Hark, hark, rejoicing's begun—
Old Mr Christopher's choked on a bun!
                    (Claude Spettigue)